CAF | ICFM

THE FUNDRAISING SERIES

LEGACY
FUNDRAISING

EDITOR
SEBASTIAN WILBERFORCE

1ST EDITION

CW00485738

ICFM
CAF

Dedication

To my wife, Phillippa

The fundraising series

Trust Fundraising Anthony Clay (editor)

Corporate Fundraising Valerie Morton (editor)

Fundraising Strategy Redmond Mullin

Series editor Stephen Lee

© 1998 Charities Aid Foundation and Institute of
Charity Fundraising Managers

Published by:

Charities Aid Foundation
Kings Hill
West Malling
Kent
ME19 4TA

Tel +44 (0)1732 520000
Fax +44(0)1732 520001
Web address http://www.charitynet.org
E-mail cafpubs@charitynet.org

Institute of Charity Fundraising Managers
Central Office
Market Towers
1 Nine Elms Lane
London
SW8 5NQ

Tel +44 (0)171-627 3436
Fax +44(0)171-627 3508

Editor Andrew Steeds
Design and production Eugenie Dodd Typographics
Printed and bound by Bell & Bain Ltd, Glasgow

A catalogue record for this book is available from
the British Library

ISBN 1–85934–055–5

Acknowledgements
Butterworths, for permission to reproduce the chart on 'Rights on Intestacy',
pages 154–5, taken from *Wills Probate and Administration Services*.

Cancer BACUP, for permission to reproduce items taken from its will-making
guide on pages 179–80.

Richard Radcliffe, for permission to reproduce Tables 12.1 and 12.2 on pages
126 and 129 respectively.

Contents

The fundraising series

Fundraisers have always been among the most forward thinking in their willingness to share technique and experience. It is, therefore, surprising that, while books describing successful fundraising campaigns abound, no attempt has previously been made to establish an 'accepted body of literature' explaining fundraising activity as a whole within one series of volumes.

This is precisely what **The fundraising series** seeks to do.

Each volume is complete in itself, concentrating as it does on a key element within the fundraising 'marketing mix'. Taken together, the volumes that comprise this series will provide a comprehensive survey of existing fundraising practice, identifying, analysing and explaining the breadth of fundraising experience currently available.

The titles in the series are not intended as fundraising manuals but as fundraising textbooks that identify and explain accepted fundraising practice within a coherent framework that may be easily translated back to the workplace. These 'working textbooks' are to be used by academics and practitioners alike. To this end, each title addresses the core fundraising competencies contained within the Certificate of Fundraising Management qualification awarded by the ICFM.

Each title explains the historical development of the fundraising practice in question and identifies the philosophical and theoretical context within which current work practice is grounded. The main body of each text is then devoted to an analysis of current activity and the identification of key learning points to guide future action.

Without a willing cohort of fundraising specialists prepared to share their skill and experience with others this series would simply not have been possible. My thanks to each of them: together they have created the first, comprehensive series of fundraising textbooks anywhere in the world.

Stephen Lee
Series editor

List of contributors

Helen Atherton and Liz Batten are joint owners and directors of Crossbow Research. Both have many years' research experience and are hands-on researchers who conduct many of the qualitative interviews themselves and organise all the questionnaire design and analysis on quantitative projects.

Virtually all Crossbow's research is in the not-for-profit sector, the vast majority for charities. Crossbow's clients include a range of charities, such as the British Heart Foundation, RSPCA, the Samaritans, Arthritis Care and the British Diabetic Association.

Anthony Clay has spent the last 10 years working in fundraising consultancy (having previously worked for 10 years as Head of Fundraising at the RSPB). He has helped more than 60 charities with cost-effective voluntary income generation, especially the promotion of legacies. A director of FR & C Ltd, he is also chairman of the Institute of Charity Fundraising Managers (ICFM) Professional Practices Committee and editor of the *Trust Fundraising* title in this series.

Crispin Ellison has had over ten years' hands-on experience in both legacy marketing and administration and is a former Chair of the biennial charity/solicitor initiative, WillAid. He was also the originator and initial development co-ordinator of the legacy software package, First CLASS. Crispin is currently legacy manager at British Heart Foundation and assists in running the Legacy Marketing Group.

Derek Humphries is managing director of Burnett Associates. He lectures and consults for organisations around the world and has directed the strategic and creative elements of campaigns for over 100 causes – from local hospices to Greenpeace International. He is a founder member of the Institute of Direct Marketing and a former vice-chairman of the ICFM.

Andrew Mortimer is a partner in the firm of Stone King. Previously with a city firm, Allen & Overy, he now heads Stone King's Private Client Department, advising clients on wills, probate, trusts and tax planning (UK and non-UK), and also charity law. The firm has a strong charity practice, advising charity clients both in the south-west and nationally. It has particular experience in advising schools and religious charities.

Hector Mullens retired from Barnardos at the end of 1996 after 45 years working in the charity. For the last 27 of those years he was in charge of the section of Barnardos that looked after all legacies. He also co-chaired the Annual Legacy Officers Meeting for many years with Derek McEwen, his counterpart at the Imperial Cancer Research Fund (ICRF).

Richard Radcliffe is currently director of development at Smee & Ford, where he is responsible for creating legacy marketing strategies, researching, developing and running training seminars and courses, and researching and developing new ideas and techniques to maximise legacy income for charities.

Prior to joining Smee & Ford, Richard ran the legacy campaigns division at Buzzacott for eight years. Before that, he was in senior fundraising and marketing positions with the Charities Aid Foundation (CAF), the Order of St John (St John Ambulance and St John Ophthalmic Hospital in Jerusalem) and the Multiple Sclerosis Society. He is chairman of the ICFM Convention and a Fellow of the ICFM.

John Rodd made a career change in 1988, moving on to database marketing and the application of IT to fundraising and marketing problems. Previously he had worked as a manager with the national Blood Transfusion Service and deputy director of fundraising at Save the Children Fund (in charge of central appeals, committed giving, legacies, advertising and market research).

John Rodd & Associates, a consultancy specialising in the application of information and information technology to any part of the fundraising or marketing process, was formed in 1990. Since then, the consultancy has worked for a wide variety of not-for-profit organisations in the UK, Eire, Europe and America. The firm also specialises in market analysis and offers legacy and legator analysis as one of several services offered.

Tom Smith, Director of External Affairs at Smee & Ford, is an experienced speaker and trainer on legacy-related topics, and has been closely associated with the ICFM's legacy training. He writes, designs and presents many of Smee & Ford's own legacy marketing seminars – and is currently involved in legacy education programmes for several national charities. He is also the founder and editor of *Codicil*, the only legacy-specific publication available to the voluntary sector.

Tim Stone is Legacy Administration Manager for the Royal National Institute for the Blind (RNIB), having previously worked with the trustee department of a major high street bank. A member of the Society of Trust and Estate Practitioners (STEP), he is currently setting up an Institute of Charity Legacy Officers.

Sebastian Wilberforce is legacy fundraiser for the RNIB and an associate member of the ICFM. He is also chair of the ICFM working party on the ethics of legacy fundraising, and a member of the inter-charity Legacy Marketing Group. He previously practised as a solicitor (in wills, probate and charity law) and was a parliamentary research assistant. He has written articles for a variety of publications and contributed research to four books, latterly *Running a Charity* by Francesca Quint (Jordans, 2nd edn, 1997) which is a legal guide for the layperson. He is also assistant secretary of the Charity Law Association.

Foreword

An intriguing thought I have had while reading this book is that just 15 years ago it would not have been possible to produce it at all. In those 'dark' days most fundraisers (and certainly legacy fundraisers) would never have been persuaded to divulge any information or knowledge of what they were doing to anyone else, sometimes even those within their own charity. This especially applied to legacy officers, who would keep their cards so close to their chest that they would make the strongest 'Chinese wall' look like a paper bag! And anyone who believed that a consultant would share *anything* would have been quietly locked up!

It therefore reflects great credit to fundraisers that over the years they have not only been increasingly willing to share their knowledge and expertise on various topics but have recognised that, by doing so, they have actually been able to achieve more than the sum of their respective parts. It is no mere chance that the increasing profile of legacies as a valuable source of charity income, and the increase in work done by many charities in this field, have coincided with a noticeable decrease in the number of people in the UK who die intestate. Nevertheless it also has to be remembered that, for all the supposed sophistication of fundraising techniques, the proportion of charitable wills has not dramatically increased either.

The role of the ICFM in promoting the culture of shared knowledge cannot be overlooked or underestimated. Bearing in mind that this book is just one of a series on various types of fundraising, it is a rich reward for both the Institute and CAF that so many leading lights in the legacy world have both given their time and, more importantly, shared their expertise so willingly.

Legacy Fundraising is absolutely required reading for anyone remotely connected with this wonderful form of voluntary income. For someone just starting out on the legacy road in a tiny new charity, serving an 'unpopular' cause, with no budget, no known supporters and no staff, this book is a must, since it will amply demonstrate how obtaining legacies is possible even in this 'impossible' scenario. For the established fundraiser in a large charity with a long legacy track record, reading this is also a must, as it is packed with ideas as to how it is always possible to improve legacy income, and, at the same time, may help to bury for good some of the shibboleths that have pervaded legacy marketing for all too long.

If you thought that the subject of legacies was synonymous with quill pens, dry and dusty Dickensian offices, expensive lawyers with their complex legal jargon, even more expensive fundraising techniques, very long-term and dubious returns, and, above all, long mournful faces and that 'D' word, this book will set the record straight. For a start, it covers every topic in good old plain English, for which all contributors are to be warmly congratulated. It also offers an enormous variety of choice for small and large organisations on how to tackle the various parts of the legacy fundraising cycle; its messages are unarguably clear, and it is chock full of genuine and highly relevant case studies.

I can only say that, having spent all my working life in the legacy world, this book taught me that, if I ever harboured the faint and occasional idea that I might have little to learn on the subject, I laboured under a massive delusion. Every chapter has made me realise how much I still have to learn from my colleagues and friends. They are all experts in their fields and they have combined to give you, the reader, the best and clearest insight into the subject that has ever existed. If you do nothing else, spare the time to read *Legacy Fundraising*. It will be the best and most rewarding couple of hours you will have ever spent.

David Ford
Director, Smee & Ford

Preface

I am particularly pleased to have been given the opportunity to edit, and contribute to, this book. To my knowledge, this is the only detailed study of legacy fundraising techniques available and the first book to be published on the subject since Michael Norton's *Legacies: a practical guide for charities* (Directory of Social Change, 1983). As more charities have focused on the revenue to be gained (or protected) from legacy fundraising, so the need for a book like this has increased. Indeed, as Tom Smith makes clear in Chapter 1, there is great potential for all charities in this income stream.

This book addresses the different scales of legacy fundraising activity that are possible for all sizes of organisation. It seeks to help medium-sized charities in particular but also takes small 'budget-less' organisations into account, since even they can raise funds from legacies.

Fundraisers with all levels of legacy fundraising experience are to be found in that range of organisations, including some who have no experience at all. Meeting their needs in one volume is not easy, and, if at times the level of this book appears simplistic, I hope readers will be tolerant. They will know that legacy fundraising is a specialist area of fundraising, and for the experienced practitioner too there is much within these pages to think about.

I have sought to be comprehensive in the coverage of this book and as much as possible to produce a practical, 'hands-on' or 'how-to' manual, with pure theory included only where necessary. Legacy fundraising techniques are still developing, particularly in the use of the telephone, and in the development of a code of practice.

Part 3 gives fundraisers some useful knowledge of the law relating to wills and related matters, how to administer an estate and what options exist for appointing executors.

Interspersed throughout the book are some donors' views on giving legacies to charity. I am grateful to Stephen Lee for suggesting this theme and for finding and interviewing these donors. What they say provides a thought-provoking (although admittedly selective and unrepresentative) perspective on the subject.

My aim in gathering together contributors has been to get the very best – the experts in the field they address – although this should not be taken as the reason why I have written four chapters myself!

A number of terms are used throughout the book that will be familiar to most involved in legacy fundraising but not to those new to the activity. There is therefore a 'Glossary of terms used' at the back of the book (p 179) which gathers together both legal terms related to legacies and non-legal terms specific to legacy fundraising for charities.

That word – 'charities' – in turn requires further explanation here. It is used as a shorthand for all types of organisation to whom this book is relevant. These include organisations that are registered charities and those charities that are not required to register. Into this latter category come, for instance, scout groups, charities connected to the armed forces, some smaller religious charities and charitable housing associations. The word is used to denote organisations that are not legally charitable (for example, Friends of the Earth, Amnesty International and Greenpeace) and voluntary organisations which are not charitable but have a public-benefit purpose, like self-help groups and small community associations.

A number of acknowledgements are due. I am grateful to David Moncrieff of CAF and to Stephen Lee of ICFM for giving me the chance to make the contribution to the voluntary sector that this book represents, and for their advice and guidance. The further editorial assistance of Nina Behrman and Andrew Steeds has been much appreciated. Thanks for their support also go to Barry Gifford, RNIB's Director of Finance, to Valerie Morton, RNIB's Head of National Fundraising, to Stuart Case of Pell & Bales, and to Nina Botting of Shelter and Fiona Hesselden of UNICEF both for their help and also for their permission to reproduce materials in my chapter on the use of the telephone. I am also grateful to Issy Howells, formerly of UNICEF for her help, and to Pat Wise and Sally Roff from NSPCC and the Suzy Lamplugh Trust: they helped me in particular with the personal safety aspects of face-to-face fundraising. Tim Stone, from RNIB, made a valuable input to my Chapter 16. All other contributors, and those who helped them with their chapters, deserve a special thanks; my wife, Phillippa, does too, for putting up with my absences from the stove for too many an evening and weekend.

Introduction: What is legacy fundraising?

Richard Radcliffe

This introduction gives an overview of legacy fundraising which explains the need to integrate legacy fundraising fully into the main fundraising plan: a legacy is, after all, purely a mechanism for giving. It highlights aspects peculiar to legacy fundraising as against other methods of fundraising from individuals, and indicates where the similarities lie. Legacy fundraising is not as arcane a discipline as some might suppose. The crucial point is made early in these pages that legacy fundraising is possible for all charities, regardless of size of budget.

A tentative definition

Legacy fundraising is a method of fundraising that uses the mechanism of making gifts in wills as a marketing tool. It is a method of *planned* giving – as are payroll giving and covenants. As with all other methods of fundraising, the role of the mechanism is secondary to the message that the charity should be communicating – the case for support.

The message about the charity and its work is a way to the potential legator's heart, and the mechanism is a way to the potential legator's assets. Legacy fundraising is the only form of planned giving that combines the two. The other methods of giving usually access only day-to-day revenue or bank accounts.

Legacy fundraising has one large incentive for potential legators which is that, when they make their gifts, no funds leave their bank account or investment portfolio. They wake up in the morning with a deserving glow, and as wealthy as they were before they made the gift in their will.

Key ingredients of successful legacy fundraising

Effective legacy fundraising relies upon identifying and developing two-way relationships. A relationship has to combine the heart with the mechanism through:

- careful, detailed research (internally and externally);

- effective expression of the need for legacies and the case for support;

- an effective strategy that enables the best use of all possible 'vehicles' to carry a legacy message;

- a well-defined structure to help fulfil the strategy – including training trustees, staff and volunteers (if your charity has any) to help spread the word;

- a financial plan and budget that are well thought out and include all the resources identified in the strategy (especially a good database software system);

- a wide range of methods for building relationships with agreed target audiences;

- effective evaluation procedures so that there is a programme of constant improvement.

Often the structure of a legacy campaign might be similar, though not identical, to a big-gift campaign. However, legacy fundraising must be fully integrated into the main fundraising plan, because it is only one of a range of mechanisms for giving. Some donors may want to give small sums regularly through a direct-marketing programme but may also want to plan ahead and pledge a legacy.

What is unique about legacy fundraising?

It is worth considering some of the aspects of legacy fundraising that are peculiar to it:

- A legacy is a one-off gift – you can't die twice.

- Despite the fact that a legacy is likely to be the biggest gift ever given by the individual concerned, legacy fundraising is not carried out in exactly the same way as a big-gift campaign.

- Legacy income is unpredictable, but it is becoming slightly less so for charities that have a history of receiving legacies. Research into 'wealth at death' is increasing, and improved methods of data capture and more advanced pledging techniques help identify possible levels of future gifts.

- Trustees find it easy not to invest in a legacy campaign, because it is possible that the results will only come through after they have finished serving on the board. However, good results can show within two years.

- The charity should be careful about asking for funds for a specific project, in case funding is complete by the time the legator has died (in such cases, the 'trust' between the legator and the charity cannot be fulfilled, and the legacy can then be contested).

- Many fundraisers tend to be reluctant to ask people for a legacy because they feel uncomfortable about mentioning death. Research shows, however, that 98 per cent of elderly people do not mind mentioning the word 'death'. Indeed, a sensitive approach and the occasional spark of humour can break the ice and help people to talk about it – this deployment of sensitivity and humour is unique to legacy fundraising.

- Finally, because the legator has to die for the charity to receive the legacy, all other types of fundraising from that individual stop at this point.

What does legacy fundraising have in common with other types of fundraising?

It is also worth considering some of the aspects of legacy fundraising that it shares with other types of giving:

- Legacy fundraising is cause led.

- It must be integrated into the main fundraising plan, together with all other methods of fundraising.

- It needs just as much planning, thought and creativity as any other type of fundraising.

- As with other methods of planned giving, it is tax efficient.

- If you ask for legacy pledges in the right way, you will get them, because many people like giving legacies.

Past approaches to legacy fundraising

In the past, legacy fundraising relied on promoting the mechanism (making a will) rather than the cause, and no relationship was developed between the charity and the pledged legator. In fact, charities often remained in total ignorance of the fact that a pledge had been made – which hardly promoted a positive relationship with legators who had promised to be extremely generous and who might, handled differently, have given more during their lifetime!

This mechanism-led form of fundraising produced a number of myths that are sometimes supported by so-called 'facts'. One such, which you will hear from some charity fundraisers, is that 'we do not know 80 per cent of our legators; we cannot trace them on our database'. This kind of comment should always be treated with caution: it could be that a charity that says this is in fact admitting that its system for capturing data is inadequate; it may well also be the case that the legator actually knew *them* very well.

CASE STUDY THE IMPORTANCE OF DATA CAPTURE

A married woman died in a hospice. When, years later, her spinster sister died, she left a legacy to that hospice, in recognition of the excellent care it had provided for her sister. The legacy did not, however, mention the sister who had died earlier. The hospice had no trace of the spinster sister, because she had not been a regular supporter. As far as the hospice was concerned, she did not exist – because her surname could not be matched to the person who had been cared for, her married sister. The spinster sister could not afford to give any substantial sum when she was alive and had only given funds in occasional street collections.

If legacy fundraising is to be effective, detailed data capture is essential and should ideally include the whole family, so that relationships can be identified and warmed up. In this case, if the hospice had been aware that the sister had made her pledge, it could have said a large 'thank you' to her at the time that she made her pledge. This might have pleased the sister, and she may even have increased the size of her legacy. As with all relationships, the benefits would have been two-way.

Because its main concern was to promote the mechanism, legacy fundraising used to be relatively simple. Many large national charities advertised regularly near the 'births and deaths column' of national newspapers. A few thousand charities advertised in the annual Christmas supplements of the legal press, such as the *Law Society Gazette*. Regionally active charities advertised in specialist press items such as *Will to Charity* or *Charity Choice*. Mailings of a legacy leaflet were carried out, and some charities included a reply tick box on the response mechanism of their general mailings, saying 'Please send me more information about leaving a legacy to charity X'.

And that was that – it worked, but only to a limited extent.

Present and future options

Times are changing, and more creative approaches are being taken, with different options for different kinds of charity.

The choices open to any charity will naturally depend on the size, budget and resources (including volunteers) of the organisation, its database or the number of its supporters, how long it has been in existence, the type of charitable activity it performs and the level of public awareness of this activity.

The remainder of this book will offer plenty of food for thought within a well-structured framework; there are lots of ideas that cost very little to implement, for a large return and minimal risk. Many of the examples given below (and which will be developed at greater length in the rest of this book) cost virtually nothing, and most of them may be carried out by both small and large charities. The size of the organisation only affects the way in which they are fulfilled.

Some options for activity

Newsletters

If your charity has a newsletter, then develop a co-ordinated string of legacy messages: describe what has been achieved by legacies in the past, present the testimonial of a current pledger, and give examples of possible future needs. A legacy message should appear in every newsletter.

Posters

If your charity is relatively small, and 'budgetless', design a series of A4 legacy posters on your computer and ask to have them displayed in church halls, community centres and other public locations.

Articles

Get a well-known, or local, solicitor to write an article in the local press (preferably close to 'Make a will week' – see p 93 for further details) on the benefits to an individual of making a will and the benefits to charities of charitable bequests (an example of your own charity can be used).

Annual report and accounts

Include a running 'footer' (a message at the bottom of each page) requesting legacies, together with a stapled-in response mechanism or postcard which includes requests for more information on legacies.

Exhibitions

Do you have an exhibition stand or board? Include an example of what has been, or can be, achieved by legacies and, ideally, a testimonial from a current pledger. It can also be useful to include some humorous examples of legacies to help attract attention. Display the boards at a local exhibition or a local shopping or community centre on a Saturday morning.

'Making a will' guidelines

Ideally develop and print these internally, so that changes in inheritance tax levels can be updated at minimum cost. There is no need to go into the mechanics of making a will at length in the legacy leaflet itself.

Talking to groups

Whenever giving talks to community groups, include a request for legacies – some of the statistics in this book make good ice-breakers – just make sure the approach is appropriate for the audience (as with 'direct marketing' below).

Training volunteers

Volunteers will need training in public speaking if they are to promote legacies at public gatherings. They can learn how to express the need for legacies and the case for support. Maintain training programmes to keep up enthusiasm for asking for legacies at community groups.

Direct marketing

Much will depend on your direct-marketing budget, strategy, type of charity and size of database. For instance, a small Christian charity could develop a modest direct mail campaign around Easter with a message from a local Christian leader or 'celebrity'. Larger-budget charities will have many different options. As an example, committed givers could be segmented in terms of age and geo-demographics, and you could mail all 59–64 year olds on the need to look at their wills now that they are approaching retirement (and take the opportunity to wish them a happy one).

Telemarketing

Many people feel that unsolicited phone calls from charities are an infringement on their privacy. However, if it is well planned, controlled and executed, telemarketing is a useful follow-up technique to small, segmented direct-mail programmes and can lead to face-to-face talks.

Face to face (one to one)

Face-to-face legacy fundraising can be very beneficial – it helps build the closest relationships – but it can also go badly wrong! Training of those involved is vital, but the response (from good campaigns) is worthwhile.

Other options

Other vehicles for legacy fundraising include advertising (local and national), leaflets, in-memoriam cards (distributed to funeral directors), telephone helplines (for legal advice or information about methods of giving), a video to support public talks, and television and radio 'news' items or messages.

Conclusion

Remember, legacy fundraising can be very effective because people like to give through legacies. Expressing your charity's need for legacies, however, is a message that needs to be put across at every opportunity.

Structures and strategy

Why seek legacies?

Tom Smith

This chapter describes the sizes of legacies, who leaves them and who receives them, and is therefore particularly useful for readers who have to make the case for legacy fundraising to sceptical trustees. It also highlights the value of sector benchmarks against which the performance of one's own charity in legacy fundraising can be measured. Measurement of this kind may bring to light idiosyncrasies to do with one's own organisation, the cause it works for or its supporters, and may also reveal discrepancies with other similar organisations that may prompt you to a greater understanding of your own legacy fundraising.

The profile of a typical legator

Research*, in all its forms, has enabled charities and the voluntary sector as a whole to build a picture of a typical charitable legator. She (for two-thirds of charitable legators are women) is something like this:

- She dies in her early eighties, having made or amended her final will within a few years of death.

- She lives alone – in a retirement or suburban area, her spouse or partner having pre-deceased her by several years.

- Her estate is valued at approximately £138,000, her home being the prime asset.

- She is cash poor but asset rich, often living on a fixed income.

- Her charitable donations (late in life) are small or non-existent.

* Smee & Ford has researched wills and estates in England and Wales emanating through the Principal Probate Registry in London and its associated district probate registries. This research is supplemented by results of legacy marketing questionnaires procured from charity clients.

- Her will names three charitable organisations from different cause areas.

- The most popular causes she will choose in her will concern health care, animals and physical disablement.

- If she leaves pecuniary legacies, they are likely to be valued at £3,200 each – and, if residuary, £24,000 each.

- Her chosen charitable beneficiaries usually reflect the experiences, relationships and influences gathered over a lifetime – and are very likely to include the wishes of her late spouse or partner.

- She – like only 39 per cent of other charitable will makers – names a solicitor as an executor in her will.

- She is very unlikely to tell her chosen charities about their forthcoming legacies – hence the 'pennies from heaven' syndrome.

('Pecuniary legacies' and 'residuary legacies' are defined in the Glossary of terms used, p 179.)

Most frequently favoured charitable causes

In recent times a feeling of depression has often been expressed about legacies. Fundraisers often identify it as a crowded market-place – with too many charities vying for 'their share' of what is per-ceived, by some, to be an area of diminishing return. Yet more and more charities are hopping on to the legacy bandwagon. Charities continue to plough the tried and tested furrows of legacy marketing, while legacy booklets, advertising, videos, pledge acquisition, direct mail and other techniques have not disappeared. A glance at your favourite mid-market Sunday newspaper will reveal a wealth of legacy offers – all very similar, all promoting their free legacy litera-ture.

Market shares

It is difficult to assess legacy market shares in income terms, because details of legacy income figures are publicly available for relatively few of Britain's many thousands of charities. *Dimensions of the Voluntary Sector*, published by the Charities Aid Foundation (CAF), is a valuable yardstick for measuring the voluntary income of the UK's top 500 charities, including that from legacies. The 1997 edition revealed that (after SORP) £565 million in legacies alone was shared by the 500 – and just 76 charities accounted for 84 per cent (£476 million) of that income. To add an even sharper focus, the top ten legacy-earning charities raised nearly £238 million from this source. Seven of those, it could be argued, were highly legacy dependent, because at least 50 per cent of their total voluntary income came from legacies.

Legacies, of course, are not limited to the few hundred largest charities. Smaller, lesser-known charities often find themselves the beneficiaries of huge unexpected legacy windfalls – and several thousand charities inherit legacies, to a greater or lesser extent, every year. The total annual market for all charities receiving legacy gifts probably exceeds £1 billion.

It has been possible to assess market share in legacy numbers for almost ten years. Research undertaken in 1996* found that 84,337 individual charitable legacies matured in that year. Closer scrutiny revealed that 53 per cent of those charitable legacies were pecuniary, and 47 per cent residuary. Table 1.1 illustrates the cause areas most favoured by charitable legators in that year, ranking the causes in order of popularity. It is worth noting that the positions of the causes have been much the same since research began: health and care charities have always been the most attractive proposition for legators, while arts-related voluntary organisations have been the least attractive.

The 1996 research showed that 277,000 people had each left estates valued at £5,000 or over in Great Britain. Collectively those estates were worth almost £21.6 billion. Of these people, 218,000 had made wills – yet only 29,000 (13.3 per cent of those who made wills) had left provisions for charities within them. Most of those charitable legators (83 per cent) had estates valued at between £5,000 and £200,000.

Those 29,000 people who chose to make charitable provisions in their wills made an average of three legacies each (usually for different charitable causes), and 47 per cent made or amended their final will within three years of their death. Of all charitable legacies, 60 per cent were left by those who lived in the south-west, the Home Counties, East Anglia and the Greater London areas. The three peak months of will-making activity were March, October and November.

Sixty-six per cent of all charitable legators were women – and, on average, each possessed an estate worth £138,000; the average estate of a man leaving a charitable will was valued at £166,000. Non-charitable wills of women and men had average values of £74,000 and £85,800 respectively.

* The research was undertaken by Smee and Ford Ltd, as part of its annual survey of estates and charitable legacies.

TABLE 1.1 TOP 14 CHARITABLE CAUSES FAVOURED BY LEGATORS, 1996

Charitable cause	Legacy numbers	Percentage of total
Health and care	19,417	23.0
Animals	12,603	14.9
Disabled people	7,964	9.4
Religious	7,017	8.3
Cancer research	6,638	7.9
Medical research	6,550	7.8
Armed services and marine	5,290	6.3
Children	4,846	5.7
Aged	3,118	3.7
Overseas aid	2,931	3.5
Environment and conservation	2,753	3.3
Education	1,525	1.8
Learning difficulties	920	1.1
Arts	588	0.7
Total	**82,160**	**97.4**

Note The remaining 2,177 legacies – 2.6 per cent – were either discretionary in nature or unclassified for purposes of this research.

Research data on wills and estates in Scotland became available for the first time in 1996; figures before that date are only available for England and Wales. These show that from 1992 until 1995 approximately 1.2 million people died leaving estates of £5,000 or more in England and Wales. They left behind fortunes amounting to a colossal £84 billion – and only a tiny proportion (roughly one in seven) made wills that included anything for charities!

The rise and fall of legacy values

The respective overall numbers of pecuniary and residuary legacies are now almost equal – but this has not always been the case. Fifteen or twenty years ago, 80 per cent of charitable legacies were pecuniary in nature – and some of them, by today's standards, were low in real value. Legacy marketing, if nothing else, has certainly impressed upon the donor the value and potentially enduring nature of residuary charitable bequests in a healthy economic climate.

Research from 1988 shows us that 'average' legacy values were worth more then than they are now. Average charitable pecuniaries in 1988 were worth £2,500 each and residuaries £25,000. Similar research in 1993 showed that pecuniary and residuary values had both fallen – to £1,700 and £21,000 respectively.

In 1995 there was a resurgence in pecuniary values. At £3,200 each, they had nearly doubled on the 1993 figure – but residuaries continued to decline steadily to an average value of £20,000 each.

In 1997, average pecuniary values held steady at £3,200 each, but there was evidence of a real growth in average residuary values, which now approached £24,000 in value. However, this figure is still £1,000 less than the 1988 figure – nearly ten years previously.

The depreciation in residuary legacy values in the past is likely to have been caused by adverse conditions in the property market, because real property is often a significant component in the make up of a residuary estate. A buoyant property market equates to booming residuary values, and in periods of uncertainty these values become vulnerable. For this reason, charities may continue to attract similar numbers of residuary legacies but, because their value is reduced, overall income reduces significantly. Given this state of affairs, charities are constantly under pressure to produce more legacies for similar or even diminishing returns.

Table 1.2 looks at the average values of pecuniary and residuary legacies made to 14 different types of charitable cause in 1997.

Recent trends

Management and financial controllers, in any kind of organisation, tend to be focused on bottom-line results – cash. However, legacy promoters need a vision that looks beyond legacy values, because legacies (especially residuaries) are almost always affected by circumstances beyond their control: rising or falling property prices, or boom or bust at the Stock Exchange.

Legacy fundraisers need to keep a keen eye on up-to-date trends and analysis. The number of charitable wills and legacies passing through the various probate systems is a strong indication of whether members of the public are more or less inclined to support charities through their wills at a particular time.

TABLE 1.2 THE AVERAGE VALUE OF PECUNIARY AND
RESIDUARY LEGACIES MADE TO DIFFERENT CHARITABLE
CAUSES, 1997 (£)

Charitable cause	Average pecuniary (£)	Average residuary (£)
Health and care	2,820	21,856
Animals	1,600	13,920
Disabled people	2,555	31,667
Religious	4,655	19,298
Cancer research	2,990	27,145
Medical research	3,780	18,783
Armed services and marine	1,130	16,269
Children	3,200	21,522
Aged	2,370	28,302
Overseas aid	1,280	23,397
Environment and conservation	1,295	29,415
Education	8,550	30,483
Learning difficulties	4,920	18,464
Arts	3,470	26,384

Research into proven wills and estates acts as a window into historic patterns of legacy giving. Although it is not possible to access every will, data has been accumulated on all proven wills in England and Wales valued in excess of £5,000.

This research indicates that consistent, if not spectacular, growth in legacy numbers occurred between 1991 and 1994, in spite of the prevailing economic conditions (see Table 1.3). A downturn occurred in 1995 – but figures given for 1996 may hint at a revival. It is too early to be either gloomy or ebullient with regards to the long-term future of legacies.

Conclusions

The Henley Centre for Forecasting has drawn attention to growing concerns over the future reliability of legacy income. It is reported that some of these concerns relate to historic, social and economic changes which have made an impact on the wealth patterns of the

TABLE 1.3 PATTERNS OF LEGACY GIVING IN ENGLAND AND WALES, 1991–1995

Year	Number of charitable legacies (in wills of over £5,000)	Pecuniary legacies (%)	Residuary legacies (%)
1991	65,037	52.9	47.1
1992	70,053	52.2	47.8
1993	72,370	51.5	48.5
1994	73,604	52.3	47.7
1995	71,643	52.3	44.7

older age groups. The declining numbers of spinsters, well noted for their propensity to make charitable bequests, reflects the tail end of a process started in the First World War. In contrast, the growth in home ownership which started in the 1960s is likely to have a positive effect on legacy income which will eventually feed through to the patterns of inheritance.

Other factors militate against a growth in legacy income. An example is the propensity of legacy pledgers to spend more of their assets in later years on a more active retirement and, subsequently, on their own continuing health care. People are living longer and are more aware of the fact that they may need to provide for themselves in later life, rather than relying on the state to do so.

Research highlights one vitally important fact – a relatively small number of legators provide a vast income stream every year. For legacy fundraisers there are still great opportunities to increase the level of wills that contain legacies to charities, thereby increasing the income to the sector from this source. Active, efficient legacy marketing, undertaken with sensitivity towards potential legators, is likely to provide the only realistic means by which bequest levels can be increased in the future.

A donor's perspective 1

This Case Study is one of five 'donor's perspectives' that are given in this book. These perspectives are extracts of taped conversations undertaken by Stephen Lee, Director, ICFM, with a variety of individuals between May and July 1997. To ensure anonymity, all reference to the individual names and charities has been removed from the transcript.

No, I haven't got a will. We talked about it once – well, actually, we had a row really, because I just thought of it one day when we were on holiday, you know how these things come into your head sometimes? And so we 'discussed' it, and that was the end of it really.

I suppose it's one of those things that you don't really like to think about, and if you don't think about it at the right time and in the right way it's easy just to push it to one side. That's not to say that I don't know that it's important, though; after all, we've got three kids and some grandchildren now and, you know, really we are not getting any younger. We do give to charity. In fact, we seem to give more and more these days because there are so many appeals and government seems to be doing less and less. We don't give large amounts, mainly because we couldn't afford it, and we much prefer to give to what we want to, when we want to, so we get involved much more at a local level through friends and family.

We've never really considered the idea of making a gift to charity in a will, although, now you mention it, I have seen some stuff from charities from time to time saying we should consider it. I think our first concern is going to be about making sure that the house is all right, that the kids and the grandchildren are looked after and, you know, if there is anything else left – which there probably won't be – we really haven't even given any thought to what we might do with it.

That's not to say that I don't – we both don't – know that making a will isn't important. It is. And talking to you just reminds me that we have really got to sit down and do it. I suppose that we have to see a solicitor or something like that; I have no idea how much it costs or what it actually entails. If you asked me whether I'd give money to charity in my will, the real answer is I have never really thought about it, but I think in the first instance we are going to be much more concerned about looking after the house, the kids, the pets and each other. I'm not against giving money to charity and I know they do really do important things, but to be honest I have just never really thought about it.

CHAPTER TWO

Ethical issues

Sebastian Wilberforce

Legacy fundraising raises many sensitive issues, principally because of the implicit connection with death. This chapter seeks to address some of these ethical matters.

Is legacy fundraising acceptable in principle?

This chapter discusses some of the.ethical issues surrounding legacy fundraising and provides guidance on how to deal with them. Ethical issues can be quite difficult to distinguish from matters of best fundraising practice, a fact which will be reflected in the discussion that follows.

The Introduction described a legacy as a mere mechanism for supporting a charity. It is perfectly reasonable to bring to supporters' attention the possibility (even desirability) of expressing their support for the charity by this means. Reservations about legacy fundraising centre on the trigger for such a gift, which is death.

As people age, so they realise the proximity of their own end. Legacy fundraising is targeted precisely at those people who, by reason of their age, are more aware of their impending death than others.

Elderly people face the idea of their death, if not with equanimity, at least with an acceptance of its inevitability. Many look positively on the idea of getting their affairs in order, even to the extent of wanting advice about whether to draw up, and where to keep, detailed lists of their assets and their whereabouts. There is no reason why fundraisers should not profit from this on behalf of their charities; indeed it could be said to be a valid part of donor care to inform such individuals of the legacy option as a final gift. Many individuals who were unaware of this option welcome being told of this means of expressing their support for a favourite cause.

Particular issues

Does the subject of death come up?

The subject of death does come up, usually during face-to-face work and in the sense of 'when I'm gone', or when husbands or wives contemplate whether they are going to die before or after their partner.

If fundraisers have to refer to death, they are best advised to do so in a matter-of-fact way, remembering that that is how most elderly people view the event. Elderly people appreciate a direct attitude that uses words like 'dying', or 'death' or 'dead' rather than euphemisms: this is particularly the case with people who have been bereaved. Euphemisms such as 'passing on' or 'on the other side' should be used only with care, and it is positively inadvisable to use more jokey euphemisms such as 'when I've toppled off my twig', even if the person being spoken to uses such terms.

Promoting the giving of legacies to charity

A variety of different media can be used to promote the giving of legacies to charity. All promotional material needs to balance the duty trustees have to maximise the income of their charity with the potential legators' freedom to provide for their family and other concerns.

The location of legacy fundraising publicity should be appropriate to the nature of the cause concerned, the content of the fundraising message and the likely disposition and circumstances of the recipients of that message. It is hard to envisage a situation, for instance, when it would be appropriate to place legacy leaflets in the accident and emergency department of a hospital.

All fundraising materials used by third parties (including volunteers and branches) should ideally be agreed beforehand by the charity concerned. In practice, of course, this can be difficult (where for instance a branch is autonomous).

All fundraisers have to have a working knowledge of the relevant codes of practice governing matters such as advertising and direct marketing published by the industry bodies.

The fundraising message

The fundraising message must exaggerate neither the need for which legacy gifts are sought, nor the impact that a legacy can have on addressing that need. It must also not be simplistic in its portrayal of either the need to be met, or the effect of dying without a will.

Particular care needs to be taken when seeking funding for a particular project, as will be explained later (see pp 160–2).

The message must also be based on factual evidence and be capable of corroboration. It must not exploit the vulnerability, credulity or security of the target audience, nor must it seek to induce a response based on fear or guilt.

Vulnerable target audiences

Fundraisers need to be alert to the signs that someone is, or might be, vulnerable, and they should never exploit anybody's vulnerability. Elderly people are often vulnerable, and legacy fundraisers will encounter such individuals more often than other fundraisers, particularly as fundraising technique becomes more personalised and one to one.

Any of the following individuals may be particularly vulnerable:

Users of the charity's services Care should be taken to present the fundraising message in a way that does not deter such people from using the charity's services, for instance by allowing the perception that there is a hidden cost in doing so.

Terminally ill Charities may decide that legacies should only be solicited from terminally ill people on a face-to-face basis, in the presence of a third party (such as a family member or staff member of the institution where he or she is being cared for) and in light of a careful assessment of the individual's state of mind. Care should be taken to assess whether an approach leading to the face-to-face encounter is appropriate in the first place. Fundraisers need to be particularly careful as to how their actions could be interpreted by friends or family of the prospect. Honesty and openness are essential.

Bereaved Fundraisers need to be aware of the grieving process, and of the time it can take for grief to subside. If they encounter a bereaved individual, they need to be careful not to become the focus of the anger such a person is likely to feel, or to have it projected through them on to the charity. Similarly they should not exploit loneliness and vulnerability. Having said that, the gratitude of a charity, properly expressed, for the compassion shown by the deceased in leaving a legacy to a charitable cause may indeed be a comfort to the bereaved.

Next of kin of legators In addition to the above, the fundraiser needs to let a decent interval of time pass before seeking to develop next of kin into pledgers. This period should at least encompass the time it takes for the size of the legacy to the charity to become known (if not actually paid over), and for any factors relevant to developing the next of kin to come to light during the administration. Such factors may include resentment on the part of the family that the charity has benefited at all.

Fundraisers need also to be aware of the test in law of the mental capacity to make a will (although this is not, strictly speaking, an ethical matter). This is particularly relevant in face-to-face fundraising. When making a will, individuals must be 'of sound disposing mind': what this means is that they must understand the act of what they are doing in making a will, and the effects of doing so. They must also understand the extent of the property which they have to dispose of, and comprehend the claims to which they ought to give effect.

Undue influence

This subject overlaps with the previous topic. Fundraisers need to be aware that gifts in wills can be set aside if a claim of undue influence is successfully established. They need to recognise when a person's weak health or state of mind could render him or her susceptible to influence in an unacceptable manner, and to know when to back off from asking for support. In cases they consider borderline, fundraisers should make a written note of what passed between themselves and the individual and of matters they consider might be relevant to the issue of susceptibility to influence. They should retain these until the individual dies and only destroy them on obtaining legal advice as to whether or not to do so.

Project funding

A difference between legacy fundraising and other fundraising is that, whereas with the latter gifts can be earmarked for particular projects, the scope for doing so with legacies is very limited. This is because a legacy is a future gift whose date of receipt cannot be accurately predicted. It may be paid out many, many years after the will containing it is written, at a time when the recipient charity may not be performing the activity in question, or may not need the funds for that purpose. A later chapter discusses the situation if a legacy is received for such purposes (see p 161).

Prospects should be advised to make their gift for the general charitable work of the organisation, thereby freeing its hands to use it as seems most appropriate when received. Alternatively, a gift can be made for the organisation's general charitable purposes with the wish expressed (no stronger than that) that it be applied for a particular project or service. The charity has the scope to apply it in that way if it can, and if that project or service requires funding, but otherwise to use it in some other field of its work.

Getting the legacy written into a will

Providing standard wording for gifts to a charity (drafted by a lawyer) is common practice and entirely acceptable. Similarly, it is permissible for legally qualified charity employees to write wills for their client group, where doing so is a pure service and no fundraising is concerned.

If the testator wishes to include a legacy to the charity then, as a general rule, the charity should decline to write the will. Ideally, the testator should be persuaded to go to a solicitor who is not connected with the charity, to prevent allegations of undue influence on the part of the charity or want of knowledge and approval on the part of the testator. Unfortunately, there are individuals who insist that the charity write the will (or pay a solicitor's fees for doing so) if it wants to receive a proffered legacy.

Systematic campaigns that offer free wills to the public (with the charity paying the solicitor's fees) in the hope that legacies to the paying charity may result are to be seriously discouraged. Although, strictly speaking, this activity is permissible in law, the Charity Commission (which is expected to publish formal guidance on the subject in 1998) advises individual charities to think very carefully before embarking on this type of venture.

Providing individuals with lists of solicitors from whom to choose a firm to write their will is entirely in order, but charities need to be careful not to be seen to be in any way endorsing the quality of workmanship of those firms. Charities should not have anything to do with will writers who do not possess at least the training in will writing and the qualifications of legal executives or solicitors.

Motivations for support

In England and Wales the individual is entirely free to dispose of his or her estate as he or she wishes, subject to legislation such as the Inheritance (Provision for Family and Dependants) Act, whose provisions are discussed on page 156.

Sadly, a recurrent motivator for giving legacies to charity is a desire to disinherit a relative. Where a charity knows during the lifetime of the testator that this is a reason for a bequest it should at least advise the individual to review his or her will regularly, to ensure that it still reflects his or her settled intentions. Internal family politics can be notoriously complex and subject to change, and, wherever possible, fundraisers should not get involved in them. They should advise the testator to seek his or her own professional legal advice, and record that advice in a letter, keeping a copy on file.

Face to face

A number of issues arise from face-to-face work, which are discussed in greater detail in Chapter 12. With lonely supporters it can be difficult to draw the line between business and social involvement, particularly if the fundraiser likes the individual. If the fundraiser wishes to see the supporter socially, it is very important to consider at the outset the potentially negative consequences for the charity of the social relationship going wrong.

In the same context, charities need to have a policy covering legacies that are granted to fundraisers themselves by supporters, and to include this in the fundraiser's contract of employment.

Conclusion

The sector is in the early days of grasping ethical issues and identifying guidelines. It is vital that fundraisers have the most up-to-date recommended practice, and to this end the ICFM established a working party on the ethics of legacy fundraising. The working party, which first met in January 1997, consists of legacy fundraising practitioners drawn from a cross-section of organisations, a representative of the Charity Commission, and the Director of ICFM. Its deliberations will lead to a code of practice on legacy fundraising issues, which should be published towards the end of 1998.

Acknowledgements

The author wishes to acknowledge the contribution made by his colleagues on ICFM's working party to the development of his thoughts in this area. He is particularly grateful to Richard Radcliffe, Eileen Hammond (Appeals Director for the Shaftesbury Society) and Alan Hammond (Legacy Officer for the Institute of Cancer Research) for their comments. The views contained in this chapter should not be taken as a distillation of the final and considered view of the ICFM, nor of its working party.

A donor's perspective 2
Family member of a benefactor talking about her parents' will

Well, when we found out I was really very upset and hurt. Mum and Dad have always been involved in doing things in the local community, and after Vic, my father's friend, became blind, Mum and Dad both got really involved in helping to organise the local blind society – but I never thought anything about it, let alone that they would give what I sort of feel is our money, somewhere else.

We were just talking after lunch one Sunday with the whole family present, when the subject came up, and Dad said that there was a will but that the principal beneficiary was the local blind society. There was this sort of stunned silence – Mum and Dad were embarrassed by it, and so were all of us. 'Oh,' I seem to remember was my initial response, because I just couldn't understand why they had done it.

I know that it's really important to them and I know that they do get an enormous amount of satisfaction out of the work that they do with the blind society, but, you know, family is family, and it really has been very hard to come to terms with.

No, I don't think my sister or myself have put my parents under any undue pressure as a result of knowing, although the subject has cropped up once or twice and I suppose, if I am honest, I am still trying to get them to see some sort of sense. If not for me, then at least for the kids. At the end of the day I know that it's about what they want and I know that we don't really have any choice but to accept what they intend to do. But I do feel angry towards Vic and the blind society, and even though I do give some money to charity and my husband volunteers locally, I think both of us are now really against the whole notion of charities and legacies because it does cause upset. Yes, we do have a will and, no, we haven't made any provision in it for charity, and I don't think we will do so either. I know that sounds awful when you say it like that, but I really feel wills are about families, not about charities.

CHAPTER THREE

Including legacies in your fundraising strategy

Richard Radcliffe

This chapter, and the following two, develop the themes (foreshadowed in the Introduction) of putting together a legacy fundraising strategy, ensuring that you have the structure in place to fulfil it, and making an effective case for support.

The place of legacy fundraising in an overall fundraising strategy

A charity's legacy fundraising strategy will depend on the size of the charity, the amount of time it has been in existence, the public awareness of the charity, the other methods of fundraising used and the budget and resources available. However, all strategic, and business, plans should have a balanced approach in terms of risk, investment and return. Each method of fundraising may have different risks, different cost ratios, different response rates and different timetables; some may have very general target audiences (eg public collections), others very precise target audiences (eg social events) – but many people who have an existing relationship with your charity will, given the opportunity, want to give in more than one way. Full integration is vital: a potential legator does not belong to a different species from a direct-mail donor.

Having said that, different charities face different challenges in the attempt to increase legacy income. For instance, AIDS charities generally have a younger supporter profile than the longer-established national welfare charities, and this makes legacy promotion more difficult. A different challenge may be faced by a local arts charity, which is unlikely to have received legacy income because arts organisations have not generally promoted legacies, and their supporters tend to be focused on attending events for their own enjoyment or to entertain friends or clients. Educational bodies (such as public schools) often have no fundraising volunteers, but they do have many former pupils who currently tend to be asked to help with an occasional capital gift appeal only.

All charities in need of funds can generate legacy income. If the charity is going to give itself the best opportunity to succeed, however, it must not implement legacy fundraising as a separate activity – only the mechanism of giving is different. Legacy fundraising has to be integrated into the overall fundraising strategy.

Planning a legacy strategy

The planning and implementation of a fundraising strategy will vary from charity to charity, depending upon a number of factors, not the least of which is the size of the charity. A major national or international charity with substantial resources might carry out a considerable amount of internal and external research and then implement a substantial campaign using hundreds of volunteers; a small charity with a budget of a few hundred pounds, and a small supporter base, might use legacy fundraising techniques only as a secondary vehicle for seeking donations within their overall fundraising strategy, as a test to benchmark future expectations. One such approach might be merely to include, in all response mechanisms, a tick box with 'I want to pledge a legacy to Charity X' and thereafter to mention the need for legacies in all newsletters.

Nevertheless, a strategy is a strategy, however large or small, and the following section is broadly applicable to all charities; some very small charities may pick and choose which elements they would like to use.

The size of legacy gifts

There is a common misconception that legacy gifts are late and 'big' gifts. This is by no means always the case. Many pecuniary legacies are very small (though none the less welcome for that), while residuary legacies are usually big gifts and should therefore be prominently requested. However, if legacies are promoted only as big gifts then it is likely that many potential legators will be put off. It is also important to realise that the pledge of a small legacy is not necessarily the end of a donor's involvement in your charity, nor even a guarantee of the final legacy.

The role of the whole organisation

Legacy fundraising is not the sole responsibility of the fundraiser or chief executive. Everyone has a role, but if that role is to be fulfilled effectively then it will be important for you to educate everyone about the facts of legacy fundraising.

Almost invariably trustees will not understand legacy fundraising, and neither will many senior managers. However, there is an extremely strong case to be made for developing a legacy campaign: the average legacy figures (see Chapter 1) represent a powerful argument in themselves, and legacies also tend to be unrestricted (general) funds and can therefore increase the long-term financial security of a charity. Trustees are in position to protect the income and assets of the charity, and legacies are probably the most cost-efficient way of increasing the assets of the charity in the long term. Ask to present the 'world of legacy fundraising' to trustees and give them the facts – call it 'The dead give-away', and they won't forget it!

Devising the strategy – a brief overview of the legacy fundraising cycle

For medium and large charities a legacy campaign should be based on the legacy fundraising cycle (see opposite).

Smaller charities can follow this structure, but in far less detail. All charities should test the market place in some way.

A legacy strategy should dovetail with the business plan of the charity. For instance, the effect of a new legacy campaign is likely to begin showing results in two years, and the full impact will be felt in four to five years' time. The overall business plan of your charity should not,

therefore, rely on major legacy income in Years 1 to 3. Predicting legacy income is uncertain, and it should usually be seen as 'an extra'; only large charities with a long history of receiving considerable legacy income can make any sort of prediction – and even that is dangerous. As legacy fundraising techniques develop, it becomes increasingly clear that current donors should be a primary target audience.

When developing a strategy, the first action to take is to develop a group of those who might prove to be keen (or who are keen). This group will vary from charity to charity, but as a general rule the following at least should be included: the fundraiser (who chairs the group), one or more trustees, a non-fundraising member of staff (eg a nurse for a nursing home, a doctor or consultant for a research charity, an environmentalist for an environmental charity), a member of the finance department, a beneficiary (although perhaps not for animal charities!), some regional representatives (for large regionally based charities), one or more volunteers and a solicitor.

Using this group, you should ideally research the full spectrum of internal and external conditions that will have an effect on all fundraising – including legacies. The group should start by carrying out research (as far as external research is concerned, both a PEST analysis and a SWOT analysis – outlined on the next page – should be used) and try to gather as much information as possible on past performance. It should then agree how to proceed for the future.

A thorough analysis of your charity's past performance is also essential: this is covered in part in Chapter 7. It is also important to research internal attitudes towards legacy fundraising – myths held by trustees, staff and volunteers need to be dispelled so that you have an extended army of activists who might (and should) help.

PEST analysis

A PEST analysis identifies external matters or forces within your sphere of operation:

- Political (eg will a new government enact new legislation that will affect inheritance tax concessions?)
- Economic (eg is the cost of residential care of the elderly going to reduce legacy income?)
- Social (eg people are dying older – what effect will this have?)
- Technological (eg will you be able to make a will via the Internet?).

SWOT analysis

A SWOT analysis identifies where your charity stands in your market place:

- Strengths (eg supportive trustees, elderly supporters)
- Weaknesses (eg lack of understanding of legacy fundraising within the charity, pressure of work on staff)
- Opportunities (eg more retired people moving into area)
- Threats (eg rumours of a new local competitor, or reduced net wealth at death is forecast).

Developing a strategy is a three-stage process:

- defining the strategic aim;
- defining the strategy;
- defining the tactics to fulfil the strategy.

For example, the strategic aim might be 'To increase overall legacy income by 15 per cent per year from the year 2001'. The strategy might be 'To enable all fundraising staff and selected enthusiastic volunteers to sell legacies throughout every region (or the local community) and to encourage an understanding of the need for legacies throughout the charity and its supporters. All those involved will be trained to accomplish their tasks effectively and happily and they will be supported with the most appropriate materials by October 1998.'

Targets must be set so that benchmarks can be made. By establishing methods for assessing the effectiveness of a campaign you are helping your charity improve its chances of succeeding.

A critical path analysis is a technique, and a very good discipline, which identifies specific tasks to be carried out within a given timetable and completion dates (or milestones) for each activity, to ensure that everyone involved knows what is to be achieved, by when and by whom.

Designing a legacy campaign to suit your strategy

A campaign will consist of a variety of tactics, and many different 'vehicles' will be used to fulfil your legacy campaign. The best way forward is to start by looking at every target audience with whom you will come into contact in one way or another, the message they should be receiving and the method of communication (or vehicle) for that message. Target audiences will include all or some of the following:

- trustees
- staff
- volunteers
- 'friends' or purchasers of goods
- existing donors and supporters
- those requesting legacy material
- those making enquiries of the charity
- those with a profile similar to current legators
- elderly people local to the charity
- offices of advisers (eg solicitors).

All of the above have a 'role' whether as potential legators (typically, elderly current donors and also trustees!), potential sellers of the legacy message (typically, volunteers as well as fundraisers) or someone who can facilitate legacies for the charity (typically, a solicitor). However, all these people could play all three roles, and often do. The best method of approach for each audience will need to be identified, and the appropriate vehicle for communication selected (most of these are listed in the Introduction, on pp 17–19).

Remember also that everyone will go through 'trigger points' in their lives which may make them either update their will or make their first one: such points include buying a first home, the death of a parent, retirement and death of a spouse. Each of these trigger points should be included within your total communication programme.

A combination of communication vehicles and methodologies will be needed, but it is important to do nothing in isolation – legacy fundraising must be an integrated activity. As mentioned above, a small working group should ideally be established to provide the support you will need to run and maintain a legacy campaign.

A school needed £10 million over ten years. This was to be raised by a major gift appeal to wealthy individuals in the UK and overseas, an annual major event for medium and small gifts and by establishing eight regional committees (to make face-to-face approaches and to develop better relationships with supporters). Legacies would be raised centrally and with the support of a small group of enthusiastic volunteers. The legacy budget was small, enough to produce a leaflet, train volunteers and fund a very small direct-mail campaign; all other legacy activities would be virtually cost free and fully integrated into the main appeal. The database of alumni comprised 10,000 individuals.

Following research of the school database, it was estimated that within seven years it would be possible to gain £3 million from legacies, most of these coming in Years 5–7. Age profiling of the database was easy to do because of the school-leaving date: 400 alumni, identified as being over 70 years of age, were the priority targets; a further 300, aged 60–70, were secondary targets. Any other approaches for legacies would come at the tail end of the appeal, following approaches to the 'under 60s' for covenants and one-off gifts under Gift Aid. Four volunteers, and their roles, had been identified, and the strategy was to develop a mailing programme supported by an in-house telemarketing campaign and face-to-face visits. These activities would be supported by a co-ordinated communications programme to all potential donors. The trustees were given a legacy fundraising presentation to ensure that they understood the process, the benefits, the lack of risk and the timetable. The strategy and budget were approved.

The volunteers were trained in telephone and face-to-face techniques so that each could contact 100 potential legators following the direct mail appeal. A face-to-face chat would be promoted if the potential legator desired it.

The telephone script was agreed, the mailing was carried out, and telephone calls followed. A pledge rate of around 25 per cent was achieved. However, to ensure that good relationships were maintained, legacy messages (and old school memories) were written in all newsletters, together with photographs of the school (and children) as it had been 55 years ago and accompanied by stories and photographs of the school's achievements since then. The total budget was £18,000 (slightly less than one average residuary legacy).

Half of this charity's annual £3 million of voluntary income came from legacies, but the general trend in legacy income was falling by 10 per cent per year, and external research projected a further drop until at least the year 2005. The strategic aim was to increase legacies year on year by 5 per cent from three years hence, and then by 10 per cent per year – with a particular emphasis on existing donors.

To try to design a new strategy that would motivate the trustees, fundraisers and volunteers it was decided to carry out research with these target audiences to ascertain their views on legacy fundraising. One trustee was seen as a potential legator: he was approached face to face and agreed a £10,000 legacy. A presentation was given to trustees, and the trustee pledger supported the presentation and announced his gift – other pledges were received within the next six months. Three regional meetings were established for fundraisers and volunteers. The agenda was to ascertain current views and activities on legacy fundraising, the range of activities that could be undertaken in the future and by whom, and the materials needed to support planned activities. The volunteers wanted to be trained in public speaking and to have an in-house guide so that they had every possible piece of information at their fingertips. A new legacy leaflet was also needed. Regional staff researched past case studies showing what can be achieved and obtained one current testimonial from a pledger to include in the leaflet.

The database management of the charity had to be modified so that the regions had better access to the current supporter database – especially those aged over 60. In addition, a new method of recording and reporting was established to monitor the activities of the volunteers. Public speaking opportunities at local 'elderly groups' and local community centres were identified and the materials agreed. The trustees approved the strategy and the budget, which increased by 10 per cent above that of the previous year. On-going costs were not increased.

The key to designing a new strategy, and gaining approval for it, is to enlist the trustees and others involved in the campaign. Legacy fundraising is often an isolated 'department', and if it remains so it will not gain the budget and support it deserves!

Financial costs and benefits

It is impossible to recommend a specific level of legacy income to aim for unless the charity has a long history of receiving legacies and captures the maximum amount of information externally and internally (and even then it can only be a good guess). All benchmarking and performance indicators rely on data capture, and the key is to start this as soon as possible. Pledge rates and your average legacy values (per each type of legacy) provide some benchmarks, as does detailed profiling of your database. However, an estimation of the value of the information you have captured will be possible only around four to six years later, and you will have to ensure that trustees are aware of this.

The cost of legacy fundraising is difficult to ascertain – especially when so many activities can be a cost-free part of other fundraising. However, it is probably the most cost-effective form of fundraising, given the income likely to be generated. It is important for the charity, particularly the trustees, to be aware of the benefits that legacy fundraising can provide – comparative income figures of competitors (by either size or sector) present good evidence of this.

CASE STUDY **A MAJOR RESIDENTIAL CARE GROUP**

This charity had a long history of legacy income (around £2 million per year) but investment had never taken place – legacy income had been taken for granted by the trustees. The trustees were given a presentation on the future of legacy fundraising, after which they understood that their residents' quality of life relied almost entirely on legacy income and that this income was at risk. One of the primary objectives of the charity in its new operational plan was to provide not only high-quality care but 'those little things in life' which enhanced their residents' quality of life. The cost of not carrying out a legacy campaign had become obvious. The total cost of a campaign over two years would be £35,000, or under 9 per cent of budgeted income for those two years – costs should not be mentioned in isolation from the benefits!

CASE STUDY **A SMALL MUSICAL COLLEGE, NIL BUDGET**

This charity (which had never raised funds) was planning ahead and needed to develop, over the next four or five years, substantially larger bursary funds. A series of four articles were written over 18 months in a newsletter to supporters (and were planned to continue). First-ever legacy enquiries were received during the year. A leaflet is planned when it can be afforded, and eminent musicians are being lined up to give their own messages.

Securing the support of everyone in the charity

Far from being a 'backroom activity, which talks about death and is aimed at solicitors' (a common view), legacy fundraising should:

- be fully integrated;
- talk about people's lives;
- be aimed at probably every target audience.

As such, it relies on support from everyone involved in the charity.

As has been described earlier (see p 41), one of the first steps in the development of a legacy fundraising strategy is to establish a group of people, one of whose most important functions will be to ensure that all those who have a role to play in this strategy (as donor or volunteer, for example) actually fulfil this role. The long-term success of a strategy hinges crucially on using the full potential of the people involved. Among these are the following:

Trustees

Trustees should lead by example and should therefore be seen as primary targets to pledge a legacy. A small pledge is almost as good as a large one – it still proves leadership. Trustees are often proud of making a pledge and can be excellent vanguards at the start of a campaign. Trustees should also spread the word that their charity needs legacies.

Volunteers

Volunteers can be highly enthusiastic speakers because they are so supportive of the work of the charity. Should they take on a public role they will need to be assessed in terms of their own strengths and weaknesses so that training meets their needs – they can then play to their strengths. Do not forget that these volunteers are also potential legators.

Beneficiaries

Beneficiaries (when applicable) often like having a new and important role, such as speaking in public, but often they will like to be accompanied by one of the above when carrying out public engagements (such as talks at Rotary Clubs, etc).

Everyone involved in every aspect of the strategy must know how, where and when to carry out all their responsibilities (this is where the critical path comes in), and the effectiveness of the activities carried out must be evaluated by the group so that there is a programme that constantly aims at improvement.

TOPIC SUMMARY SHOULD YOU USE AN AGENCY OR CONSULTANT TO HELP YOU?

There are many different types of agency and consultant, and each has its own specialisation, strengths and weaknesses. Almost certainly they will have experience and expertise that can help you. It is important to set out a briefing note or an invitation to tender for consultants before seeing them. It will be vital to comply with legislation, and all contracts should comply with the ICFM guidelines so that both sides know exactly what the tasks are, the length of the contract and the charges. The list of agencies and consultants specialising in legacy campaigns is not long, but the type of support you need will be available from at least one of them. Expertise can include: market research, database research, strategic planning, face-to-face training (groups and one to one), direct marketing, corporate image development, print and design – to name only a few.

All good agencies and consultants will offer a free first meeting – take advantage of this so that you can ascertain how well they match your requirements in terms of chemistry, experience and expertise. One final warning – many consultants present their ideas with a 'high profile' leader who then takes a back seat for the rest of the assignment. To avoid disappointment, ask who will be carrying out the day-to-day work of the assignment.

CHAPTER FOUR

Budgeting for, and evaluating, legacy fundraising campaigns

Richard Radcliffe

The effectiveness of legacy fundraising is hard to measure with any accuracy. However, given the current climate of accountability and the requirement on any activity to prove itself financially, funding is unlikely to be released for a campaign that has not been appropriately costed and for which some return on this investment has not been estimated. These issues form the substance of this chapter.

Establishing a budget

Having assessed your strategic options in the light of the size of your charity and its history of receiving legacies, your next step is to develop a budget. Drawing up a budget is the process through which the aims and objectives of the charity are expressed in financial terms. A budget enables management to determine whether the objectives are financially viable and provides the yardstick by which actual results are measured.

There are two types of budgets for legacy campaigns: an income and expenditure budget, and a cashflow budget.

Income and expenditure budget

An income and expenditure budget usually covers 12 months and only deals with revenue (ie recurrent income) and expenditure. This type of budget is what is usually presented to the trustees and is very simple to develop. If you are preparing your first budget, write down all income headings and all expenditure headings (you can use last year's actual income/expenditure to establish a benchmark). For the forthcoming year, look at your planned activities and allocate potential costs and income (a new or first legacy campaign is unlikely to have any income in the first year).

Cashflow budget

A cashflow budget is similar to an income and expenditure budget but is broken down month by month, thereby making it easier to assess the charity's cash situation. In effect, it is a monthly snapshot of income and expenditure.

Budgets should be completed at least six months before the end of the financial year. The final budget for the charity should be completed three months before year end.

Estimating the financial return, and the timing of the return, from legacy campaigns is very difficult and can often bias the trustees of a charity against investing in new campaigns. The first four years of a campaign (or a new campaign) are almost impossible to forecast; the effects should begin to show 18–24 months after the start of the campaign. After four years, benchmarks can be set, but they are often incomplete benchmarks.

Key questions to ask when preparing a budget

Does income cover expenditure each year?

If income does not cover expenditure for each year (for charities starting their first pro-active legacy campaign, it is almost certain that new income will not cover expenditure), then you will have to prepare an estimated five- to ten-year income and expenditure budget to substantiate your case for investment. It's likely that in 10 years legacy fundraising will be seen to have been the most cost-effective form of fundraising, but the main obstacle now is convincing trustees to start, given that the advantages may only accrue after they have finished their period of trusteeship.

Is the budget realistic?

Each charity is different; whether a budget is realistic really depends on the legacy strategy adopted and the quality of information on past performance.

Does the budget reflect internal developments, plans and policies?
Have you compared your budget to the performance and activities of other similar charities?
Do those approving the budget understand the different period of return and different types of risk for each type of fundraising?

Trustees should be presented with a risk analysis of each type of fundraising, so that they are fully briefed and can make a considered and prudent decision. There are virtually no risks in a legacy campaign: those that there are relate to either the wrong strategy being implemented or a bad case for support.

How is the budget to be monitored to ensure that the next budget will be more accurate?

What are activities actually costing you? All response mechanisms should be coded, and every response mechanism should ask for a pledge, so that a long-term conversion rate can be gauged. Any group or face-to-face talks should have a data-capture or response form for potential pledgers to complete after the talk.

Identifying and using performance indicators

Every activity should be measured, but the result of each output will have a different timetable. The first method of developing performance indicators is to develop a 'chart', so that you know what you are trying to measure. This might include:

- direct mail appeals;
- legacy leaflet coupon responses (per 100 mailed);
- telemarketing pledge rates;
- pledges per public speaking engagement.

The chart should also measure legacy income statistics and the performance of those involved. For example:

- average number of pecuniary legacies and values;
- average number of residuary legacies and values;
- number of speaking engagements per quarter per volunteer.

When you have built up your full list of items and activities, you then have to establish what you are measuring within each activity. For instance, for a direct mail campaign, do you want to measure the 'pledge rate per thousand' mailings against the cost of the mailing and compare that against the result of a public-speaking engagement? And if so, how? For most medium-sized and smaller charities (or those newer to legacy campaigns), it is worth sitting down with the finance department (and/or in-house IT person) and any consultant/agency you are using and agreeing what should be measured, so that costs per response per activity may then be calculated. It is extremely easy to gather information that is totally useless.

Conclusion: assessing the impact of a campaign

The legacy fundraising cycle ends with evaluation, without which the campaign is pointless. Has it worked or has it not? Performance indicators do not uncover the whole picture. It is likely that a new campaign will have involved many people new to legacy fundraising, and each one should be evaluated to ascertain what they considered to be the strengths and weaknesses of the campaign, in terms of activity carried out and the materials and training provided. When assessing the impact on those involved, it is worth organising both a quantitative assessment (in which you ask them to complete forms at regular stages) and a qualitative assessment (face to face) when you also put new ideas to them for the future. This should result in the next strategic paper for the trustees.

CHAPTER FIVE

How do you persuade people to leave a legacy to charity?

Richard Radcliffe

The case for support should be written once internal and external research has been conducted to establish current perceptions about various aspects of the charity. It should express the need that the prospect is going to want to buy into, and it should be adaptable to different communication methods and different target audiences.

Making the case for support

Generally, people give legacies because they know and admire the work of your charity – its charitable aims and objectives. The case for support should not be confused with the mechanism of the legacy. As mentioned in the Introduction, the message about the charity and its work opens up the potential legator's heart; the legacy mechanism opens up the potential legator's assets.

When developing your case for support you should already have carried out internal and external research so that you are aware of everyone's views of the charity, its work, its image and its needs. Indeed, the best research identifies why a relationship with your charity is worthwhile. It is analogous to getting married: you do not walk up to someone you do not really know and ask them to marry you – you need to know about one another, what motivates you both and what you have in common. It is when compatibility has been confirmed that you are in a position to ask for a hand in marriage or a legacy in a will.

You will need to present the facts and emphasise the benefits a charity gains from receiving legacies. It might be that you have to adapt the case for support for each target audience. Then you have got to plan the method of communication for putting across that case for support. The main method of communication is often the legacy leaflet, but there are many other vehicles, including newsletters, talks and exhibitions (some are listed in the Introduction).

As a general rule, the art of persuasion relies on sense and sensibility. The core details for the case for support should dovetail with the aims and objectives set out in the charity's constitution (which is a good starting point) and the latest mission statement. However, these are both general statements and can be rather indefinite. It is important to remember that a statement is going to have to be very persuasive if it is to move a person to make the effort to go and have their will made or updated – that effort is not something we do every Saturday when we are out shopping. The statement also has to be strong enough to last.

CASE STUDY **GREENPEACE**

The classic case for support was expressed in that now famous poster by Greenpeace in Australia: 'When you come back as a whale you'll be bloody glad you put Greenpeace in your will.' It says it all in a nutshell and it is applicable to all target audiences.

The case for support will be the written core statement within the campaign and will therefore have to work in many different scenarios – newspaper ads, public talks, inserts, articles, posters, face to face – and be attractive to all target audiences, including donors, trustees and volunteers.

It is all too easy to produce a case for support for legacies that sounds utterly general, the problem being compounded by the fact that you cannot ask for legacies for *particular* projects since that project might be finished or funded by the time the legator dies.

When developing a case for support, the following key types of support statement can prove invaluable:

- examples of what past legacies have achieved;
- a pledger 'going public' on their pledge and their reasons for pledging;
- examples of the type of work for which legacies might be needed in the future.

Consider also whether you should be offering a form of recognition for legators (such as inclusion on a board of remembrance), but beware of offering anything 'in perpetuity' – this can be extremely costly, if it is at all possible. It is a combination of all these statements that is likely to motivate a potential legator to go to their solicitors or executors and say, 'Do my will' or 'Make me a codicil'.

Cold, warm and hot prospects

Asking for legacies is not a one-off exercise which is mailed generally. There should be a well-structured communication programme that meets the expectations of both those who have never been mailed and those who are committed givers. Because legacies are only a mechanism, cold prospects should be tested with great care, and it should be remembered that cold prospects are potentially regular donors as well. The way in which prospects are distinguished and approached will again depend on the charity, its history, supporter profile, other fundraising activities and the media being used to communicate the case for support. Cold prospects are likely to be mass mailed with a preliminary test mailing to find out how best to 'warm up' a relationship between them and the charity. Hot prospects need a very different approach, and are often best approached face to face.

CASE STUDY **A NATIONAL ANIMAL WELFARE CHARITY NEW TO LEGACY FUNDRAISING**

This charity had no history of legacy fundraising, having been funded from a variety of membership and trading activities (ie not donations). The database profile indicated a majority of females who had little spare cash but who would possibly be asset-rich at death. The legacy campaign was confined exclusively to members and would be developed in the newsletter, then via a legacy leaflet for distribution through the regional network and, finally, a single, test, direct-mail shot. The target group were not hot prospects, because most had not previously been asked to give a donation.

Message 1 regular newsletter articles on the more emotive aspects of the work of the charity.

Message 2 what had been achieved by the charity in the past.

Message 3 the aims of the charity in the future.

Message 4 celebrity expresses first statement on need for legacies.

Legacies were not mentioned at all until Message 4. A few weeks after that message (which was also in the leaflet) the direct mailshot was carried out.

Moving from cold to hot – getting the mix right

As a general rule, moving a potential legator from cold to hot will be done as follows: mass marketing, targeted/segmented marketing, and finally one-to-one talks in person. The way you get to the one-to-one situation will depend entirely on all the particular characteristics of your charity. The best way to proceed will be to test the message and the methods of communication, because not every person likes direct mailshots and not everyone wants a face-to-face talk with you. Hospice supporters (volunteers and donors) are often much more open about thinking about their own mortality and preparing for it; supporters for arts organisations are often very different. It is being sensitive about our separate sensitivities that leads to success.

A donor's perspective 3

To be honest, I'd never really thought much at all about the need to make a will, because I've never really thought about death in that way. Looking back – and even, to be brutally honest, *while* I was going through the process of establishing my first will – the notion of making provision within it for charity was never really uppermost in my mind.

What is interesting, though, is that the initial impetus that led to the decision to make a will actually came from a charity advert in the national press. I didn't respond to the advert directly – in fact, I can't even remember who the advert was for, because there are so many of them these days, aren't there? – but I remember noticing the ad and mentioning to my partner that we really ought to think about making some sort of will.

It's interesting, the first person I talked to about it was actually my dad, believing intuitively that he would already have a will and might be able to explain the whys and wherefores to me – because he was older than me (and perhaps because I hoped I might be a beneficiary from it). It was a bit of a shock broaching the subject of his, and my, mortality so directly, but actually once we got into it, it was really quite fascinating and gave me an interesting perspective that I hadn't had before on his and my mother's own concerns and aspirations.

One of these aspirations, which I had never really thought about before, centred on a specific bequest within my father's will for quite a large sum of money to be left to cancer research. In retrospect, I suppose I shouldn't have been surprised, given that two of my grandparents died from cancer-related illness and my parents cared for both of them through a long and difficult period.

My partner and I had long, and sometimes intense, discussions, not only about the content of my father's will (!) but also about the need for us to do something about our own. In a sense, for someone in their late 40s, the whole process still seems somewhat removed, given that we both naturally assume that we will be here for many years to come. In another sense, however, talking about making a will made us both realise just how much we had to think about distributing to each other and elsewhere, should we no longer be here. But it also made us begin to think about some of the causes that we've supported on and off ever since we've known each other.

The next step was to contact the solicitor. The only time I have ever used solicitors is when I have bought and sold my houses, and so it was to this solicitor that I naturally turned first. She was really nice and told me over the telephone very quickly just how easy it was to make my will and, given that we had some concerns about making a will so long before our intended demise, just how easy it is to amend all or part of our wills as we go through our lives.

When we met her, much of the conversation actually revolved around the two of us thinking very carefully about what we wanted to do with our individual and jointly owned possessions and assets, and I must say our first and principal thoughts were really only for each other, for family and for friends.

We did, however, continue to think about some of the causes that we support. One of the real problems for us was our own recognition, through this process, that much of our support is actually transient and dictated as much by fashion in particular causes as it is by anything else. After not too much debate, because we were more concerned with ourselves and our family, we did resolve to make a gift in our wills to two charities. We were concerned, however, that we did not want to make these gifts in the knowledge that they were somehow made irretrievably and we wouldn't be able to change or amend them as our own support for causes changed over the forthcoming years. The solicitor was really helpful in this respect and showed us just how easy it is to amend our will and also explained to us the dangers and pitfalls of leaving what you call a residuary gift as opposed to a specific bequest! In the end we chose the latter option and have made two not enormous but, we think, important bequests to the causes of our choice.

It's interesting that even though the start point for all of our discussion about making a will came from a charity advert, at no point did we have any direct contact with any charity, not even the two that we subsequently made bequests to in our will. Nor have we been in contact with either of the charities since, because for us that is not the important point about making the bequest. The important thing is that we've done it and that we believe in what they are doing. Having gone through the process, I have to say we don't think daily about the content of our will or about the standing of the two bequests to charity that we have made within it. It's interesting, though, that we do take more interest now in the activities of the two organisations we intend to support. And we have continued to provide both of them with more support than we have done before, although the idea of replying to them when they contact us and give us the opportunity to talk about wills, well, frankly it just doesn't even enter my head.

CHAPTER SIX

Legacy profiling

John Rodd

This chapter discusses profiling those who have given legacies to your organisation, reinforcing the earlier exhortation that legacy fundraising and legacy administration be fully integrated so that each understands the needs of the other. In fundraising terms this is vital, since only a proportion of your pledgers will identify themselves to you in their lifetimes.

The main cases for legator analysis

Legator analysis allows marketing planning to proceed with more reliability. As with many markets, both for-profit and not-for-profit, the future customer/legator is likely to bear a strong resemblance to past ones. A key benefit therefore is better understanding of, and insight into, legators.

The application of fixed budgets can be made more effective by using analysis to focus on the most productive geographical areas and demographic targets, and to get the most from any database of living donors. A second major benefit of legator analysis therefore is the reduction in waste and the improved effectiveness of fixed budgets.

Good data is needed for analysis to take place, as is skill in the manipulation of databases and the presentation of information for making decisions in marketing. This chapter includes a listing of typical data fields. As few as five hundred records can be used for market analysis, with somewhat more being required if geographic and demographic work is to be done. In general, the skills needed for such analysis are outside the scope of most charity marketing departments.

Why profile?

Many charities would like to know more about their legators and the bequests they have made. Sadly, these important donors are dead and cannot be interviewed. However, analysis of the records they leave behind yields valuable information that can be very useful for the planning process.

By astute analysis of past bequests it is possible to:

- understand who legators were and what they left (in terms of the mix of bequest types and value variations);
- examine trends and patterns over time, thereby giving a baseline position from which to develop projections;
- establish the identity of the common competitor or 'bedfellow' charities co-named with your charity's bequests;
- identify the best and worst targeting opportunities, size your market 'universe' and grade areas of differing attractiveness;
- understand the different yields from the genders and titles across your legacy market;
- get to know the most fertile areas – concentrations of legator locations, regional and county distributions and penetrations;
- obtain demographics – profile the social class, age and wealth characteristics of legators.

KEY POINTS

What is the business benefit of profiling?

- Better targeting: location, media, lists, gender.
- Obtaining more pledges for less cost.
- Reliable planning, with guesswork replaced by facts and figures.
- Establishing norms and trends.
- Understanding the real legator market.

Data

The most important factor in legacy profiling is data. Information on bequests and the people who made them is the starting point. It does not matter, for the purposes of analysis, whether the data is stored on computer or as hard-copy records: it is, however, immeasurably better to use the former, as the data preparation of raw will data is time-consuming and costly.

Table 6.1 demonstrates a typical range of information required (this is usually stored in 'fields' in most computer database software).

TABLE 6.1 TYPICAL INFORMATION REQUIREMENTS FOR LEGACY PROFILING

Field name

1	surname
2	initials
3	gender
4	title
5	age at death
6	year of death
7	year of will codicil
8	age of will (calculable by deducting 7 from 6)

Legacy types

9	pecuniary
10	residuary
11	discretionary
12	specific
13	reversionary
14	residuary share (if other charities co-named)
15	amount received (£ value of bequest)

Field name

16	total estate value
17	bequest as proportion of estate (calculable by dividing 15 by 16)
18	address line 1
19	address line 2
20	address line 3
21	post-town
22	county
23	postcode
24	address is: private or residential (nursing home)
25	cash-donating history (where known)
26	bedfellow charities

Obtaining this information is usually possible where a charity has good legacy administration. Items like the postcode must be verified against the up-to-date postal address file as they may have been misread, or, in the case of older estates, altered in the wake of the restructuring of the postcode area. The postcode is the vital 'hook' that connects the legacy record to geographic and demographic data.

Typical analyses of legacies or legators

This section comprises some typical analyses to illustrate options for legacy profiling. They are based on real case data, but disguised to prevent identification.

Bequest mix and value variations

Table 6.2 shows the wide variation which can exist in a market of legators.

TABLE 6.2 BREAKDOWN OF BEQUESTS BY VALUE AND PROPORTION

Legacy type	Total value (£)	Average value (£)	Percentage of database	Percentage of income
Pecuniary	1,506,992	1,135	70.3	14.7
Residuary	8,609,502	15,876	28.8	83.9
Multiple*	135,648	9,974	0.7	1.3
Specific	1,932	1,137	0.0	0.0
Discretionary	2,383	1,402	0.0	0.0
Total	10,236,458	5,435	99.09	99.8

* Multiple means a will containing more than one type of bequest, for example a pecuniary bequest and a share of the residue.

The principal messages here are that residuary legacies are by far the most valuable: although representing just under a third of all bequests (28.8 per cent), they accounted for over 80 per cent of the income, a disproportionate figure that not all charities are aware of.

A key question that arises from this information is 'What are these few people like who account for so much?'

Trends and patterns over time

Establishing baseline positions enables a charity to look at past trends in legacies received, allows projections of future events and enables the charity to examine any significant variations from the norm. These can sometimes be traced back to significant bursts of promotional activity, events in the wider world (such as media-driven surges of interest following a catastrophe that thrust the charity into the limelight), or significant internal events (such as silver jubilee year).

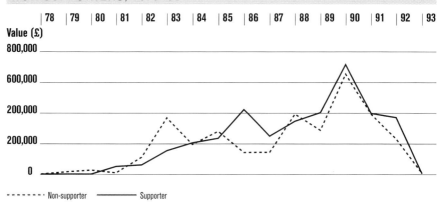

FIGURE 6.1 VALUE OF BEQUESTS FROM SUPPORTERS AND NON-SUPPORTERS, 1978–93

- - - - - - - Non-supporter ————— Supporter

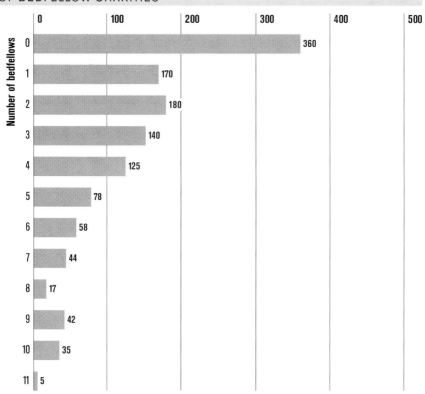

FIGURE 6.2 ANALYSIS OF BEQUESTS ACCORDING TO NUMBER OF BEDFELLOW CHARITIES

Figure 6.1 includes a further refinement, drawing a contrast between legators previously known as supporters of the charity and 'non-supporters'.

Competitor or 'bedfellow' charities

These are the charities named alongside yours in a will. Analysing data for this information can become complex unless the analyst has a classification system available to place charities in related classes (environment, overseas development, medical research, etc).

It can come as a surprise to legacy managers just how often they are treated as 'just one more' organisation on the legator's list.

As Figure 6.2 shows, only about one-third of all bequests is made solely to the charity in question. Comparison of data with norms as measured by Smee & Ford (see Chapter 1) also gives some indication of how a charity is doing in terms of market share.

In the longer term, the monitoring of bedfellow ratios over some years allows us to see if marketing activity is improving market share or not. If a charity has a reasonable set of historical data, the ebb and flow of bedfellow ratios can be determined with ease.

Identifying best and worst targeting opportunities

There is an '80 : 20' rule in almost every business: around one-fifth of the customers account for four-fifths of the business (sometimes called Pareto reporting, after its originator). In legacy analysis, it is a good move to identify the élite few and then single them out for analysis and comparison with the overall base.

The example illustrated in Figure 6.3 shows clearly that the lion's share of income (69.8 per cent) is attributable to just one tenth of the charity's legators. With this analysis, we are in a better position to establish the most and least valuable types of legator, and to see where they came from, what socio-economic group they belong to, their gender mix and so on.

Gender differences

It is widely held that women leave more to charities than men and that their greater longevity makes them more frequently the ultimate legator.

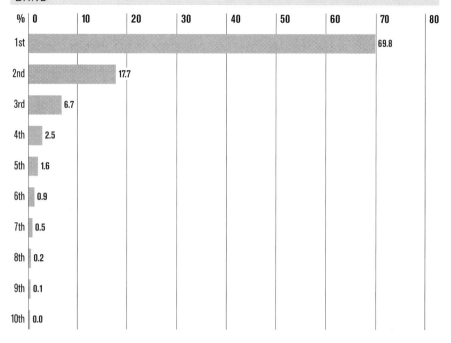

FIGURE 6.3 PERCENTAGE VALUE OF BEQUESTS, BY INCOME DECILE BAND

%	0	10	20	30	40	50	60	70	80
1st								69.8	
2nd	17.7								
3rd	6.7								
4th	2.5								
5th	1.6								
6th	0.9								
7th	0.5								
8th	0.2								
9th	0.1								
10th	0.0								

TABLE 6.3 GENDER OF LEGATORS: ANALYSIS BY GENDER AND INCOME

Gender	Number (%)	Total value of legacies	Average value of legacies	Contribution by value
Female	1211 (63)	£7,138,500	£5,924	66%
Male	699 (37)	£3,634,500	£5,200	34%

In the analysis shown in Table 6.3 it is clear that, while there is no great difference between males and females in the average value of their legacies, females make a vastly greater overall contribution to income. Legacy planners must make of these data what they will, but charities are more and more being recommended to pursue different communication strategies for men and for women.

Geographic variations

Older people tend to move to retirement areas in their later years. This will come as no surprise to many legacy managers, but what is surprising is the fact that this knowledge is not used in targeting resources to the areas of greatest potential. Charities commonly have records of a hundred thousand living donors, and many have five hundred thousand or more: targeting legacy fundraising by location can make budgets go further and for longer. Figure 6.4 shows a simple breakdown of legator location, done without the use of maps.

Figure 6.4 shows only the location of legators in the top 50 per cent of bequests by value. It shows that the market in this case is highly segmented geographically.

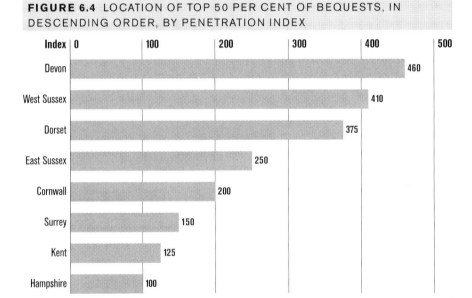

FIGURE 6.4 LOCATION OF TOP 50 PER CENT OF BEQUESTS, IN DESCENDING ORDER, BY PENETRATION INDEX

There is not scope in this chapter to show map-based reports, but, by using databases attached to geographic information systems, it is possible to obtain a bird's-eye view of locations, create thematic maps of wealth by territory and isolate the most fertile areas. In many a legacy manager's office you will find a map of the UK with any number of coloured pins on it. High-quality geographic analysis takes this a stage further and in addition allows 'drill-down' into the underlying data.

Demographics – profiling for social class, age and wealth

So far this chapter has looked at legators using data provided by legators themselves, but, geography apart, we have no insight into their position in the wider community. Were they wealthy, middle class or poorer than average? And who bequeathed the most? Should we be aiming at the upper sectors of British society, or are there significant pockets of legacy wealth elsewhere? And where are those in the top 20 per cent located? Are they in the most prestigious groups or not?

One method of demographic profiling is to use the postcode of the legator to link into one of the several geo-demographic systems available. Figure 6.5 shows the variations that can occur in a legacy file. It is based on one of the best-known of such systems, the ACORN™ system*.

ACORN stands for A Classification Of Residential Neighbourhoods, and is an all-purpose classifier of consumer markets. The A to F bands are graded by wealth, with A standing for 'thriving' (the wealthiest people in Britain), B for 'expanding' (the 'Barratt Homes' part of British Society), C for 'rising', D for 'settling', E for 'aspiring' and F for 'striving'. (These are the CACI descriptions of the bands.)

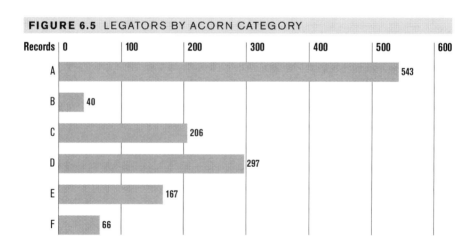

FIGURE 6.5 LEGATORS BY ACORN CATEGORY

This analysis shows strikingly how the wealthiest stratum of society is highly penetrated: people in the top residential class are most likely to leave legacies. An index of 543 tells us that ACORN Type A is nearly five and a half times more fertile for legacies than average. There is a significant secondary segment far lower down the social scale at D, which has almost three times the average penetration.

* ACORN is a registered trademark of CACI Ltd, London.

Table 6.4 demonstrates the far richer picture that may be revealed by demographic analysis than plain, unadorned internal data. In this table, A2, a subset of the most affluent group in Britain (Group A), is very under-penetrated, but another, A3, is many times more 'potent' than A as a whole. (There were few legacies from ACORN B in this analysis, so Group B is not represented in the table.)

TABLE 6.4 LEGACY INCOME BY BEST ACORN GROUPS

ACORN group	Description	Count	Penetration	Value
A1	Wealthy achievers, suburban areas	222	158	£1,567,900
A2	Affluent greys, rural communities	21	89	£138,307
A3	Prosperous pensioners, retirement areas	157	553	£1,784,576
C6	Affluent urbanites, town and city areas	63	246	£498,514
C7	Prosperous pensioners, metropolitan areas	66	276	£277,443
C8	Better-off executives, inner city areas	77	189	£499,554
D9	Comfortable middle agers, mature home-owning areas	166	127	£980,100
D10	Skilled workers, home-owning areas	38	36	£104,431

These measures may easily be tied to value, gender and geographic segments to derive a far clearer picture of who a charity's legators were, graded by their contribution to overall legacy income.

In many studies, it is not uncommon to find as much as three-quarters of legacy income generated by just a few of the ACORN groups.

Skills and tools required for this analysis

The skills required to create the analyses outlined above are generally beyond the marketing department of a charity, although the growth of database manipulation in the sector may be changing this. The graphs and charts shown above started out as extracts from a FoxPro database, created from either hard copy data capture of clients' wills, or as a dump from a legacy administration package such as First CLASS or even some in-house, tailor-made systems.

These data are then read into SPSS, the standard statistical package. This contains a number of pre-set reports that are then converted into user-friendly graphics. These generally form part of a report which looks at the shape and characteristics of the past legacy market.

Conclusion

Analysis of legacies or legators can be carried out with relatively small numbers of legacies. Successful reports with significant impact on planning have been generated from as few as 500 records. This is not enough for demographic studies, since the penetration analysis is meaningless with such small numbers; the best studies are possible when there is data from two thousand or more records.

Data is the key to successful legacy analysis. The quality of legacy administration is very varied, and the hardest job of all is the initial capture of hard-copy data from piles of dusty files – the end result is well worth the effort!

Legacy analysis yields a mix of insights. Some simply, but crucially, confirm beliefs already held. It is unwise to base a long-term strategy on guesswork, and the type of analyses illustrated above aim to minimise the need for guesses.

The real benefit of legacy profiles is the accurate targeting of future campaigns. It is the simultaneous reduction in wasted effort coupled with finely tuned targeting that makes legacy-promotion budgets go furthest.

Research to inform strategy

Liz Batten and Helen Atherton

The previous chapter focused on the way the dead can inform a fundraising strategy; this chapter explains how to research the living – another key element in putting together a fundraising strategy. Given that the research that fundraisers will be qualified to do for themselves is limited, the chapter usefully concludes with advice on using a research agency.

Who leaves you legacies?

Success in legacy fundraising, as in many areas of fundraising, often comes from doing 'more of the same': in other words, legacy fundraisers can target people who match those who have already left a gift. The question of 'who leaves you legacies?' can be asked projectively; it can be addressed to people who are currently living, about whether they *might* leave a gift, and why. The question can also be asked about people who are already dead.

The living people a charity might research could include supporters, volunteers, the general public, solicitors and known pledgers. To understand more about legators and their motivations, a charity could research the executors, the solicitor and the family.

For all of the above types of people, the answers to these questions could be derived from market research. It is worth noting at this stage that, although wills and legacies are relatively private subjects, they are not taboo for most people, provided the research is sensitive. In all the legacy research they have conducted, the authors have never experienced any problems in obtaining the information they need.

Desk research

Although most of this chapter concentrates on market research, some information can be derived from desk research, once a will has been executed. A charity should be able to check the names of benefactors against its own database, to ascertain whether legacies come mainly from people who were known to the organisation (eg supporters or volunteers) or from previously unknown sources. Although the latter may form a large proportion of some charities' legacies, it is hard to know how to plan for them. Hence, the majority of this chapter concentrates on the former category – known contacts – who can be targeted and communicated with.

It is important to check against the database to find out what type of supporters tend to leave legacies. This will help with future targeting, by providing information that will help a charity to replicate previous successes. For example, discovering that the majority of legators are members of a charity, rather than donors, would help to inform the legacy marketing strategy. This information can be gleaned from desk research.

Desk research does have a role to play, but this role is limited, and it cannot tell you what persuaded someone to include a charity in their will. Nor can it tell you why some people seem reluctant to make a bequest (clearly, you cannot break down those barriers until you know what they are). This kind of more detailed information can come only from market research, which is the focus of the remainder of this chapter.

Who are your supporters?

Some charities have a clear picture of the demographics of their supporters and of the reasons why they support the organisation. However, other charities know very little. A lack of knowledge may not matter much in the early days – say, if a charity grows out of an emergency situation and appeal – but it certainly *will* matter as time goes on.

In donor acquisitions, it is essential to know the demographics of your best prospects. For the whole fundraising programme, it is also vital to understand your supporters' motivations for giving. Do they respond rationally or emotionally to your cause? Do they have some personal connection with the cause or do they 'buy into' it as a worthy but remote crusade?

Arguably, if a charity cannot answer this kind of question (and increasingly, they can), the success of any appeal programme will be a hit-or-miss affair. The same is true of a legacy campaign. In order to run a successful campaign, it is essential to understand the demographics of the supporters. For example:

- How old are they?
- Are they 'family' types?
- Are they home owners?
- Do they already have a will?

These are fairly basic facts to be gathered. However, supporters' attitudes and motivations also need to be understood. The sorts of question that charities often ask are:

- Where does our organisation 'fit' in supporters' charitable giving?
- If they have included this charity in their will, why have they done so?
- If they have *not* included this charity in their will, why not?
- How do they feel about pledging?
- Do they perceive that there are 'benefits' to them in giving by means of their will?

The answers to these questions can help charities to refine their message and the means by which they communicate with supporters. How you ask the questions will depend on a variety of things:

- the sample size needed;
- the types of supporter to research;
- the mix of questions to ask;
- why the research is being conducted.

The main research methodologies used to research attitudes to legacies are postal and telephone (quantitative techniques), and face-to-face in-depth interviews and focus groups (qualitative techniques).

Quantitative research will provide hard numbers, such as: 'X per cent of your supporters have a will', or 'Y per cent are older, single women'. However, qualitative research will be able to delve more deeply into motivation and attitude. For example, in a postal survey, a member may not admit to wanting a beautiful picture as a thank you for pledging. However, in a face-to-face interview, the respondent will be more relaxed and will often be more frank.

This book is about how to plan and execute a legacy campaign, rather than how to conduct market research, so this chapter deliberately avoids describing how to conduct each type of research. However, most people who work in these types of research will be happy to discuss their details.

CASE STUDY **POSTAL SURVEY**

A large national charity had identified a portion of its database as offering good prospects for legacies. It wanted to check that it had selected those prospects on the correct parameters and to understand whether the attitudes of the legacy prospects matched those of 'standard' donors.

A postal survey was conducted, which identified the legacy prospects as being older, more often female and more likely to be single than the standard donors, thereby validating the selection. The research revealed that the majority of legacy prospects already had a will. It was therefore more appropriate for the charity to talk to them about changing their wills and bequests, rather than about making a will in the first place. The research also identified that the samples had slightly different reasons for their support, and so future mailings could adopt a slightly different 'tone'.

Who *were* your legators?

As mentioned above, this question can to some extent be answered by checking legators' names against your charity's database. Some information may also be gleaned by contacting a legator's executors or solicitor: this can be particularly helpful when that legator was previously unknown to the charity. Although solicitors may not know the details of their legators' charity support, they may know why they left a gift in their will.

The other information that may be gleaned from an executor concerns the legator's family composition. Although it may still be true that the majority of legacies come from single, childless, women, it is important to dispel the myth that *only* such people leave legacies. By quoting examples (without using real names) of 'family' people who have left a gift, a charity may persuade other people to consider doing so.

What other questions can research answer?

Even for well-informed charities, there will be other questions that need to be asked, as a legacy strategy develops. These can include:

- How should we treat our legacy prospects?
- What communications should we send?

- What would persuade people to tell us about their gift?
- Do pledgers now want to be excluded from appeals?

Your own desk research may help to answer some of these questions. For example, can you keep a record of how much pledgers donated before and after they became pledgers? If giving has started to tail off, you may want to alter the type of appeals.

However, what desk research cannot tell you is *why* legators' donations have tailed off or how they feel about hearing from you. This is where market research can play a key role in helping you get the best from your donors.

CASE STUDY **IN-DEPTH INTERVIEWS**

A national disability charity wanted to know how best and how often to communicate with its pledgers, about whom it knew relatively little. In-depth interviews revealed that the pledgers knew very little about the organisation's work, but were keen to know more. The research also showed that the charity's existing newsletters were exactly what pledgers wanted. The charity could easily fulfil the need, and it could do so cost effectively by using materials that were already being produced.

Using a research agency

It is important to use a research company that you feel comfortable with and that has relevant experience. It is true that there are many good researchers, but the ones that are most useful to a charity are those who understand the sector. Such researchers will be able to make better suggestions about the sample, about the questions to ask, and so on. Perhaps more importantly, though, they will be able to interpret the results in context. In short, they can tell you if your results are 'normal'.

Your choice of agency should also be informed by the fact that you will ideally be aiming to build an on-going relationship with it. This does not necessarily mean working with only one company, but it is probably sensible to restrict the number of companies with whom you work. That way, the researchers learn more about your whole operation, and the 'learning curve' at the beginning of each project is much reduced.

When briefing researchers, it is worth trying to involve other relevant parties, such as your direct marketing agency, or whoever will be working with you to implement your legacy programme. This ensures that everyone knows what is going on and, again, helps brief the researchers more fully.

How do you find an appropriate research agency?

If your experience of research is limited, or you want to change to a different agency, there are a range of ways in which you can find someone. One of the simplest is to pick the brains of colleagues, both within your own organisation and in other charities.

Alternatively, you could try one of these two organisations:

- **Association of British Market Research Companies** (ABMRC) Select Line: telephone 0800 801 785 This is a free helpline, run by ABMRC, which will put you in touch with specialist researchers.

- **The Market Research Society:** telephone 0171 490 4911 This is the industry body to which professional researchers belong; it can also put you in touch with relevant agencies.

Perhaps the most important point about using a research agency is not to be worried about the cost of using one. Usually, some research can be conducted, no matter how small your budget. Give them a call and see what they can do to help. It is hard to give guidelines on cost: every project is different. However, it costs nothing to ask! Your legacy strategy, like all fundraising, should be based on the best knowledge you can acquire about potential legators and their attitudes towards your organisation.

Briefing an agency

Market researchers often work without a written brief. However, if you can provide something in writing, the project is likely to get off to a better start. Although a good researcher will be able to marshal your ideas into a well-defined project with clear objectives, it is much better if the charity starts out by stating why it wants to conduct the research, and how the results will be used.

Having said that, if you do need help with these two issues, a good research agency – particularly one with experience of the voluntary sector – will be able to help you. Depending on your experience of market research, you may already have a view about the use of qualitative or quantitative research – and a preference for one should be shared with your agency – but bear in mind that the researcher is usually best placed to make the recommendation on choice of technique.

The final point about briefing an agency is to be as open and honest as possible. It is a myth that researchers will conduct an unbiased piece of research only if you do not tell them what you want to get out of the research: any good researcher is trained to do that anyway. Research will be more thorough and valuable if you brief the agency as comprehensively as possible.

CHECKLIST BRIEFING A RESEARCH AGENCY

- Background: where are you up to now, and why is the research needed at this time?
- Research objectives: what are the key things you want research to tell you?
- Sample: whom do you want to include; what types of supporter or potential supporter?
- Methodology: do you have a view about how you wish to conduct the research?
- Questions: it is the research agency's job to compile the final list, but you may have specific topics you wish to cover.
- Outcome: how do you plan to use the research?

CHAPTER EIGHT

Forecasting legacy income

Tim Stone

This chapter suggests a number of different ways to go about the difficult task of forecasting legacy income receipts, once an income stream has begun, and explains how to calculate an average bequest value. Using this methodology, a very approximate estimate of the value of pecuniary and residuary pledges can be arrived at, which you can then use to calculate a return on investment in legacy fundraising on an on-going basis. When the type of legacy pledged is unknown, take as its value the average value of your pecuniaries. You should remember that only a number of those who leave you a legacy will reveal themselves to you during their lifetime, and you should also note if the average age of your pledgers' wills (ie the period between the last will and the pledger's death) differs from that of other legators.

Introduction

There are several reasons why a charity should attempt to forecast its legacy income:

- No business – charitable or otherwise – can operate efficiently without a thorough understanding of its cashflow. For many charities, legacies form a majority part of their funding. Even if it cannot be controlled, this cashflow should at least be forecast with a reasonable degree of accuracy.

- Many charities are now 'investing' in legacy marketing. It is very difficult (particularly over the short to medium term) to assess the benefit of a marketing campaign directly. However, it is important that, when such expenditure is incurred, it is set against the forecast of income to be received over a given period.

- Forecasting of medium- and longer-term trends enables more informed strategic planning.

This chapter refers only to residuary bequests; pecuniary gifts are usually received so soon after notification that it is almost pointless to include them in any forecast. Residuary bequests in any case form the greatest part of the value of legacies to charities.

The limitations of legacy forecasting

There are three main reasons why no-one has yet been able to produce a reliable legacy forecasting model. First, even in straightforward estates, there are several stages in the administration that will take varying amounts of time to complete. This variability makes it more difficult to estimate when the estate is likely to be distributed.

Secondly, most businesses experience a degree of seasonal variation in their income streams and use this (in part at least) to forecast future income patterns. To the uninitiated, since death rates undoubtedly do respond to seasonal factors, legacies would seem to be ideal for such treatment. However, because of the many variables involved in the estate administration process, money may actually be paid out of the estate at any time during the year, without regard to seasonal bias.

Therefore, although legacy receipts show considerable monthly variation, these variations do not respond to, or reflect, any 'seasonality'. On average, income is received more or less constantly, but in any specific year individual months can vary quite considerably from the average.

Thirdly, unless there are complex issues to resolve, most executors will have finalised the estate within a year or two of the date of death. It is therefore virtually impossible to use current cases or notifications to forecast further than 18–24 months in advance. Longer-term forecasts require a slightly different approach.

Information – the foundation of forecasting

Most commercial companies have reliable information available to them regarding recognised indicators of the health and cashflow of their business – stock in trade, invoices due, debts outstanding, and so on. However, with legacy income there are no such recognised indicators, and these have to be developed before any form of forecasting is possible. The type of information required will vary according to whether one is forecasting over the short or long term.

Short-term forecasting

Indication of the existence of a bequest

Trustee banks generally notify a beneficiary of their entitlement before a grant of probate has been issued, but solicitors are not usually so forthcoming. However, subscription to a notification service (such as that operated by Smee & Ford) should result in the charity being made aware of a bequest in its favour before it is notified of it by the executor. In the absence of such an arrangement, a charity is dependent upon the executor advising it directly of the bequest. These early notifications can be used as the basis for short- to medium-term forecasting.

The estimated value of the bequest

There is no compulsion for executors to disclose the value of a bequest, but an efficient legacy department will request at least a copy of the will and a 'statement of assets and liabilities'. These two items together should provide enough information to estimate what the final entitlement will be.

An estimate of when the bequest is likely to be received

This estimate is likely to be purely a matter of judgement for the legacy officer, based upon their experience of estate administration periods, type of administrator and type of legacy (see below under 'stock-in-trade approach').

Longer-term forecasting

Trends in the following items should be closely monitored:

- numbers of bequests – monthly, quarterly and annually;
- income receipts – monthly, quarterly and annually;
- average bequest values (ABVs).

It is advisable to use twelve-month rolling averages whenever possible for the three items listed above. This should eliminate any short-term fluctuations in the month-by-month figures and enable easier identification of the underlying trends.

Three forecasting techniques

The 'simple' approach

Although it can be criticised on the grounds that it is too simplistic, this technique can provide a very rough indication of what next year's income is likely to be.

The first step is to calculate an average bequest value (ABV). It is generally accepted that legacy income is produced from cases notified during the year prior to the one in which the income is actually received. Hence, when calculating an ABV, it is necessary to divide the amount of income received during the year by the number of notifications received during the previous year. Suppose, for example, that a charity has the pattern of income and notifications shown in Table 8.1.

TABLE 8.1 INFORMATION FOR CALCULATING AVERAGE BEQUEST VALUES

Year ended	Income (£m)	Notifications
31/12/93	5.75	245
31/12/94	6.00	250
31/12/95	6.25	255
31/12/96	6.50	260

The ABV for the year ending December 1994, £6 million divided by 245 notifications, is £24,490. For the year ending December 1995, the ABV would be £25,000 and so on.

The next step is to multiply this ABV by the number of notifications received during the current year, in order to provide an estimated figure for next year's income. The predicted result for the year ending December 1995 would thus have been £24,490 multiplied by 250, giving £6.12 million – the actual result turned out to be £6.25 million.

There are difficulties with such a simplistic approach, and it can sometimes give inaccurate results. One important shortcoming of this system is that it makes no allowance for large one-off legacies that can easily distort the income pattern and which should, ideally, be separately plotted. However, as a broad indicator, this method does have the major advantage that it is easily explained and understood.

The 'historical performance' approach

As mentioned above, the charity will probably be notified of a legacy 12–24 months in advance of actually receiving the proceeds. To produce a long-term forecast (ie over any period greater than, say, 18 months), a certain amount of trust has therefore to be placed in the fact that income will continue to be produced at roughly the same rate as it always has been. This is the fundamental reasoning behind the 'historical performance' method, which was designed to forecast (with a moderate degree of overall accuracy) up to four years in advance.

The system is based on an assumption that the amount received in total over any five-year period will be received in varying proportions in each of the five years. If income were to be received regularly throughout the five-year period, one would receive 20 per cent of the total in each of the five years. In practice, one would normally expect to receive a smaller percentage of the total in Year 1 and a greater percentage in Year 5. Given the number and type of calculations involved, this method is probably best dealt with by way of a computer spreadsheet. However, the principles behind it are demonstrated in Table 8.2 (which shows a sample of actual RNIB legacy receipts over a five-year period).

TABLE 8.2 HISTORICAL APPROACH: LEGACY INCOME OVER A FIVE-YEAR PERIOD

	Income (£)	Year income as a proportion of the five-year total
1	5,075	16
2	5,595	17
3	5,877	18
4	7,747	24
5	7,954	25
Total	32,248	100

The next step is to construct a series of such data (over a period of, say, ten years) to give some indication of trends in the income pattern. There are various ways in which one can then use this data to produce a series of forecasts. For instance, if we assume that the next five-year period (equivalent to Years 2–6 in Table 8.2) will have the same income distribution pattern as the previous five years (Years 1–5), income for Year 6 can be predicted as £9, 057 (The actual outcome for the next year in the sequence was £9,144.)

Although the degree of accuracy will obviously decrease as we look further ahead, the same basic technique can still be used to predict the income stream for Years 7, 8 and 9: £10,577, £11,894 and £12,428, respectively. (The actual corresponding outcomes were £10,580, £9,535 and £12, 088.)

The major shortcoming of this system (as will be apparent from the above figures!) is that it will never predict a 'one-off' drop in annual income. Sometimes it therefore has to be combined with a degree of informed interpretation (for example, of the trends described above under 'Longer-term forecasting') in order to produce a credible forecast. None the less, as a basis for long-term planning, it does have its merits.

The 'stock-in-trade' approach

This method is probably the most accurate of all. However, it depends heavily upon a thorough understanding of the principles of estate administration, together with a reliable degree of both historical and current data.

It involves estimating the likely value of an inheritance by combining any information gleaned from the copy will and statement of assets and liabilities. Then (because an administrator will usually distribute the estate in a series of payments rather than as a one-off lump sum), it is necessary to allocate the total value of that entitlement over the projected period of the administration.

In making this allocation, one must have regard to the types of asset involved and also to the type of administrator who is dealing with the estate. If the value of the estate is primarily contained in property, for instance, it is unlikely that the executor will be able to make any meaningful distribution until the property has been sold. On the other hand, if the deceased held a large part of their wealth in cash, then an early, and substantial, distribution should be possible.

As far as administrators are concerned, RNIB has found that, on average, banks are some five to six months faster overall than solicitors; they also tend to distribute more of the available cash more quickly. To work most effectively, the stock-in-trade forecasting technique therefore requires refinement in order to take account of these differences.

As a very rough guideline, we would usually expect to see around 75 per cent of available cash being distributed to residuary beneficiaries within nine months of a grant of probate being issued, with the balance being received some nine to twelve months later. However, each charity's experience will be slightly different and, ideally, a full analysis should be carried out of all available historical data in order to determine guidelines for the particular forecasting model which will apply to your individual charity. Table 8.3 shows an example of a draft cashflow forecast, reflecting the expected receipt of funds from two different types of estates – one (A) comprising predominantly cash, the other (B) primarily containing realty.

For a charity with high levels of legacy income (greater than, say, 200 cases per annum) this method is again most suitably dealt with by computer. Indeed, bespoke legacy administration packages are available which can automatically calculate a rolling total of anticipated legacy income from the available information according to user-defined parameters. However, for the smaller charity, a paper-based system should be just as effective.

Conclusion

Given the limiting factors of forecasting legacy income, no system is ever going to be entirely accurate. The number of variables involved renders almost impossible the task of the legacy officer who seeks to predict when, and how much, their charity is likely to receive. Indeed, an overall average accuracy rate of plus or minus 5 per cent should be viewed as exceptionally good. Even if such precision is achieved, though, there will undoubtedly be occasions when any forecasting system will be caught out by the natural volatility of legacy income. Although the methods suggested here can and do work effectively, they are not perfect. It is to be hoped, however, that this chapter will, if nothing else, prompt discussion and improvement of them.

Acknowledgements

While writing this chapter, I have drawn heavily on the expertise of my counterparts in other charities and I would like to thank those individuals who have given so generously of their time to discuss with me yet again the subject of legacy forecasting – 'the art of the impossible'.

TABLE 8.3 DRAFT CASHFLOW FORECAST FOR LEGACY A AND LEGACY B

Month	Event	Anticipated amount received
January	Start A (value = £150,000)	
February	Start B (value = £200,000)	
March		
April		
May		
June		
July		
August		
September		
October	Receive 75% of A	£112,500
November	Receive 25% of B	£50,000
December		
January		
February		
March	Receive 20% of A	£30,000
April		
May	Receive 50% of B	£100,000
June	Receive 5% of A	£7,500
July		
August	Receive 20% of B	£40,000
September		
October		
November	Receive 5% of B	£10,000
December		

Communication methods

CHAPTER NINE

Intermediaries and events

Crispin Ellison

This chapter challenges widespread assumptions about solicitors and the value of advertising in the legal press. It encourages a more sophisticated understanding of who an intermediary might be: anyone, broadly speaking, who can promote your organisation's need for legacies. In the light of this definition of an intermediary, a whole range of different events become suitable vehicles for promoting legacies, either as the sole objective of the occasion, or as one among others.

Introduction

This chapter discusses the involvement of intermediaries in legacy fundraising and outlines the ways in which legacy promotion can fit into general, and specifically will-related, events.

An intermediary is someone who can convey to a potential legator the need for legacies for a cause, but who is not paid or asked to do that alone.

Who can be an intermediary? Almost anyone:

- regional fundraising staff;
- staff in information departments in your charity;
- solicitors;
- branch members;
- will-writing companies;
- members of your charity's support groups;
- members of supportive groups, such as community groups;
- your charity's board or council members;
- volunteers.

Intermediaries

The sections that follow consider the advantages and disadvantages of using different types of intermediary.

A charity's regional fundraisers

A number of charities include legacy promotion within the role of regional fundraisers, which can work well where there is good training and monitoring. Of course, most regional fundraisers have 'real' income targets to achieve – 'real' in the sense of hard income that has to be achieved *this* year. They may truly support the need for increased legacy income but, when push comes to shove, their priority – and, for many, their motivation – is getting money in today, not in five years' time.

Some charities have therefore set up schemes where the fundraiser is credited with, say, a proportion of the current year's legacy income or with a notional credit of some kind. These are not always easy to operate but they can help to ensure that legacy promotion work is valued.

A number of fundraisers are quite terrified of bringing up the subject of legacies because of the connection with death. Yet, legacies to charity are all about life – making possible life-enhancing treatment, giving hope to damaged lives, even, in the case of some charities, saving lives – and some regional fundraisers will be able to convey this entirely naturally, including legacies in face-to-face conversation as a means to achieve the end. The most important task is to ensure that the individuals – paid or unpaid – have this kind of skill: it is vital.

Volunteers, including trustees

A charity's volunteers can be its greatest allies – who better to sell the cause than someone who actively supports it in their own time? An appropriately skilled volunteer (preferably one who has already included your charity in his or her will) can be a very successful legacy fundraiser. For example, it is likely that your trustees will know a number of well-connected and possibly wealthy people.

Particular care and resourcing are needed to manage, motivate and monitor volunteers. This is so important where legacies – likely to be an individual's biggest gift to a charity – are involved. Do not rely on volunteers' ability to motivate themselves, but augment it with additional care (for instance, such volunteers should receive a higher number of field visits than paid staff), proper resourcing (a computer–modem link or fax machine could ease reporting) and monitoring of progress (such as self-assessment) that is designed to avoid demotivation. Do not begrudge the extra management and resource costs that will need to be expended on volunteers: it is an investment worth making.

Groups – WIs, church groups and others

Your organisation's objectives may make association with certain groups particularly appropriate, for instance, a distinct religious affinity, community interest or concern for, say, older people. The motivation for a legacy to charity is usually closely linked to the legator's personal circumstances (particularly in later life), and what touches or has touched them. Whether or not you choose to approach community groups depends on how close a fit there is between what your charity does and what is emotionally important to individuals in those groups.

Professional will writers

When people are ready to make their wills – probably as a result of a significant event in their lives – they will usually go to a solicitor, bank or other will writer (see Table 9.1). These professionals make effective intermediaries because they are right at the 'point of sale', their advice carries weight and they have the opportunity to reach many hundreds of potential legators who are simply not known to your charity.

TABLE 9.1 METHODS USED FOR DRAWING UP WILLS, 1991 AND 1994, BY PERCENTAGE

	1991	1994
Drawn up with the help of a solicitor	77	74
Made their own will	11	15
Advised by a bank	7	5
Made by a will-making agency	–	1

Source Law Society research

Solicitors

Solicitors remain dominant in the will-writing marketplace (see Table 9.1). Many charities try to place their name before the profession, by advertising in charity directories, in the regular law journals, by mailing firms or probate solicitors, by offering wall-charts, pens and other inducements, or by sending local volunteers round to solicitors' offices.

Qualitative research carried out by Crossbow Research in 1993 indicated that:

it is very rare for a solicitor to suggest a specific charity as a beneficiary. Mostly, clients know exactly which charities they wish to remember. The solicitors feel that the client has almost always had some kind of relationship with that charity.

On advertising:

Directories are used very much as reference manuals to check the name and address of the chosen charity. The solicitor uses them simply to get the facts he or she needs to make the will 'correct'. It is only on rare occasions that either the solicitor or client uses them to choose a beneficiary.

Solicitors have almost no interest in the directory advertisements and, Crossbow Research adds, the client seldom sees the ads either. If clients cannot think of a particular charity, the solicitor would prefer to discuss their interests and help them reach a decision in that way, rather than name a particular organisation.

Some firms appear to be executors in wills more often than a recipient charity would expect. Sally Burrowes of the WorldWide Fund for Nature (WWF) comments that, while individual solicitors may not be actually commending WWF to clients, their offices are covered with WWF materials and booklets. That is, a specific partner has an interest in a particular charity's work for a personal reason, and is prepared to display their materials and promote charity bequests as a whole, if not commend a specific charity for inclusion in a will. This sort of relationship can, if appropriate, be built on to mutual advantage, the solicitor gaining a PR benefit by association with the charity's name, the charity gaining, for instance, by an agreed donation when a supporter uses that firm to make a will.

The greater prize for charities, though, is simply that solicitors should ask their clients as a matter of course if they wish to make bequests to charity. Of 25 solicitors (or legal executives) questioned in depth by Crossbow Research, just five always raise the subject. A survey carried out among 1,300 firms by Daryl Green of Jewish Care backs this up. Only a quarter of solicitors in the 200 responding firms always ask their clients whether they have considered leaving anything to charity. Yet one out of six clients do leave charitable bequests if prompted. Solicitors are reluctant to recommend individual charities to their clients – but there is a role for them to play in always asking if their clients would consider a bequest to charity.

Banks

Some banks offer direct will-writing services, and several charities have built up good relationships with individual banks. Banks tend to deal with larger estates, but the combination of small (and falling) market share and the banks' centrally governed procedures suggest that they are not a good bet as intermediaries for most charities.

Will writers and 'DIY' wills

As with licensed conveyancers, will writers have now entered the market. Most charities currently take the view that only professionally qualified will drafters should be recommended to supporters. With will writers, there are anxieties about lack of training, supervision, accountability and, particularly, lack of professional indemnity cover. Although it is early yet to assess whether problems are occurring when these wills come up for probate, Law Society research by John Jenkins already indicates that:

36 per cent of 6–10 partner firms agreed or strongly agreed with the statement 'I, myself, or others in my firm have come across several instances where we have had to sort out serious mistakes in will writing by competitive will-writing services'.

For the same reason, charities should consider with extreme care schemes that involve the individual's writing his or her own will. It is claimed that solicitors make more money out of sorting out homemade wills than by drawing up wills themselves. Besides that, there is the possibility of claims of charities exerting 'undue influence'.

Many charities therefore believe in keeping the will-making process itself at arm's length. But when you know that more than two out of three adults in this country do not have a will, can you really afford not to be involved in some sort of will-making scheme?

Events to promote will making

Some charities have formed partnerships with solicitors as a way of promoting will making while still maintaining the necessary legal distance. One of the best known of these arrangements is WillAid.

WillAid

WillAid is essentially a scheme promoting professionally made wills. It is run for one month every two years by a consortium of overseas aid charities together with some two thousand solicitors' offices. The solicitors draw up straightforward wills for no fee. The client is asked to give a suggested minimum donation which is passed to the charity consortium. Well over 60,000 clients have made or changed their wills through WillAid since 1988 and raised some £2.8 million for the consortium in donations.

The WillAid charities expect many times that figure in eventual legacies, though hard evidence for this is not yet available.

WillAid does offer an opportunity for absolutely anyone to make or change their will with professional advice at a known and reasonable cost, and therefore to include legacies to their favourite charities – like yours.

The three things that most motivate people to leave a legacy to a specific charity are: the cause, the request for a donation or support and the follow up. The cause will be specific to each charity, and the follow up is covered elsewhere in this book. The request for support is more important than the event where you make it, but it can be useful to set up 'will workshops' or advice clinics, loyalty clubs, information evenings, road shows and whatever other promotional events are appropriate to your target audience.

The Law Society's 'Make a Will Week'

The Law Society's own promotional campaign, Make a Will Week, takes place every October. The Law Society views the campaign as a public-awareness, practice-development and income-generating initiative. For instance, in 1996, it sent out a poster, leaflets and marketing advice to 13,000 solicitors. The scheme was covered in most of the broadsheet newspapers and many local papers and radio programmes. Unlike WillAid, there is no fixed fee level: it is up to individual firms to decide what their fees are and whether they wish to offer a discount to encourage will making when the event is running*.

---

* Each year's Make a Will week has a different theme. The theme of 1998's will be gifts to charity. The impetus for this has come from a number of legacy fundraisers, including the author of this chapter and the editor of this book. At the time of going to press, it seems that the week will take place later than October, possibly even in early 1999. The charity theme is a significant development for fundraising.

Paying for wills

The Charity Commission is producing guidance notes on 'Paying for Wills with Charity Funds', available from its London Office during 1998 and essential reading if you are contemplating a will-making scheme. Paying for wills should be considered with the utmost caution: there are very serious practical issues to be resolved.

The essential thing, at any event and through any intermediary, is to sell your cause, use the opportunity to describe how vital legacies are to its continuance, create opportunities for people to express an interest – and follow this activity up.

Acknowledgements

Thanks to the following for help in writing this chapter: Crossbow Research, Sally Burrowes of the WorldWide Fund for Nature, Daryl Green of Jewish Care, John Jenkins for the Law Society, Philip Black (Legacy Officer) of the Cancer Research Campaign.

CHAPTER TEN

Direct marketing, printed and audio-visual communications

Derek Humphries

The progression from direct marketing, through print communications and telephone contact to face-to-face interviews represents the ideal sequence in a legacy fundraising campaign. The increasingly sophisticated direct marketing techniques of today allow fundraisers to target more effectively the individuals they want to reach, and to maintain and develop their interest. Telephone and face-to-face contact allows a degree of interactive dialogue that no mailshot is ever going to be able to achieve. The more personal and interactive the communication between charity and prospect, the more likely a pledge is to result – provided direct marketing techniques have been used correctly to identify and start, or maintain, the process of developing the right prospects.

Introduction

The world of direct marketing is changing fast, and it is changing fast within a wider, dynamic marketing environment. Within the world of communications the talk is suddenly of expansion into global markets. Conversely, and concurrently, marketers enthuse about ever more precise targeting of individuals. As the technology available to direct marketers develops, it becomes increasingly important to use this technology wisely. The role of technology must be to enhance the quality of fundraisers' contact with individuals rather than simply to deluge the donor or potential donor with ill-targeted and irrelevant communications.

Direct marketing is growing not just for fundraisers, but for all marketers. Whether one is selling baked beans, promoting customer loyalty for a supermarket or, indeed, generating legacy income for a hospice, the emphasis is on building loyalty through one-to-one relationships. For fundraisers this means relationships that bring benefits to both the donor and the fundraising organisation. Of course, the causes promoted by fundraisers are imbued with values rather different from those of baked beans. This is one reason why direct marketing and printed communications for legacy income present particularly creative, as well as, of course, strategic and technological challenges.

What exactly do we mean by direct marketing? Direct marketing is any kind of marketing that allows the reader, the listener, or the viewer to register their interest directly. This means, for example:

- filling in a coupon from a press advertisement or direct mail pack;
- telephoning in response to a radio or television advertisement;
- responding to a telemarketing phone call.

An important consideration for the fundraiser is that direct marketing will generally allow you to collect at least the name and address of the responder. This data is the basis of a relationship with the responder and provides an opportunity for developing it, so the more relevant the data, the better. Information on age, social status, income and family circumstances can be generated through simple postal questionnaires. However, you may not necessarily be able to hold all such data on a computerised database. At the higher level of donor cultivation, detailed manual records of such information are likely to be used.

A problem for all charities is that they receive a good deal of their legacy income direct from cold prospects with whom they have had no previous recorded relationship. Legators may often be volunteers, branch members or the family and friends of beneficiaries; often they will have had a relationship with the charity that has been 'invisible' or not recorded on the database during their lifetime.

A key challenge for all organisations is to improve the data capture and 'institutional memory' (all the information held on a charity's database about the transactions between the charity and its supporters) of those people who are not currently on the records of their preferred charities. A clear record of, for example, volunteers and branch members is likely to reduce the number of legacy gifts that now appear to come out of the blue.

There is often reticence among fundraisers about appearing intrusive in asking personal questions. In reality, donors may be quite happy to volunteer information about themselves, even the vital issue of age, when asked in a sensitive and appropriate manner.

In addition to established direct marketing media, one hears more and more nowadays about 'the new media'. For most people this means primarily the Internet – a medium that provokes extreme reactions, much as did telephone fundraising and direct response television (DRTV) advertising when these media first came to the fore. The reality is that, while the Internet is not (yet) the answer to a legacy fundraiser's prayers and is certainly viewed by many, perhaps prematurely, as a fundraising red herring, it is in fact already being used by legacy fundraisers in the United States (see page 108).

The key issue, as with all direct marketing, is that different media and methods will be effective with different audiences. Moreover, different media may be appropriate at differing stages of the relationship between the charity and the prospective legator. So, for example, what is right for a 'cold' prospect may be inappropriate for an existing pledger.

The good news for legacy fundraisers is that all forms of direct marketing and printed communication – newsletters, magazines, booklets and brochures – have an effective role to play at all stages. This means conveying the right messages at the right time to help recruit, retain, convert and recognise the contributions of potential legacy donors. The aim of this chapter is to explain where certain media and methods may be more effective within the context of the challenges and opportunities facing today's legacy fundraiser. Given that each and every area of direct marketing is individually very sophisticated, the aim here is not to go into great detail, but to show how these complex disciplines relate directly to the business of legacy fundraising.

Media available in the key stages of a legacy campaign

Table 10.1 (pp 98–99) gives a brief overview of the strengths and weaknesses of media that you are likely to consider at varying stages of your relationship with 'cold' audiences, legacy enquirers, and legacy pledgers. It should be stressed that in all of these areas there is still scope for much testing and innovation.

It is also important to note that at all of these stages there is potential to identify particularly good prospects for development at a one-to-one level through either telephone or face-to-face contact (see Chapters 11 and 12).

TABLE 10.1 STRENGTHS AND WEAKNESSES OF MEDIA AVAILABLE

Key stage	Media	Strengths and weaknesses
Raising awareness	Newsletters and magazines	*Integrate the message into your broad marketing mix.* *Low or zero cost.*
	Awareness advertising	*Some larger charities have claimed a link between heavy spending on awareness advertising and an increase in legacy income. While bigger, well-publicised charities are more likely to be at the front of potential legators' minds, any causal link between the money spent on awareness advertising and legacy income would be difficult, if not impossible, to prove.*
	PR (press and broadcast media editorial)	*Some potential for placing stories in lifestyle magazines aimed at an older audience, as well as radio and TV coverage in the form of both editorial/features and as 'news' items.* *Internal PR costs only.* *Need to make staff and/or supporters available for interview.*
Generating enquiries	Press advertising	*Flexible and fast testing.* *Low cost per enquirer.* *Increasing availability of appropriately targeted media.* *Used a good deal in the past where charities were sensitive about targeting existing supporters, or where there is a desire to build up large volumes of enquirers quickly.* *Targets 'cold' supporter and perhaps the warm, but unknown, supporter.* *Being used widely as charities shift towards greater emphasis on development of existing supporters.*
	Piggy-backing inserts, mailings, etc	*Simple addition of tick boxes to existing promotions.* *Zero cost.* *Very low-key and discrete – therefore no space for detailed explanation and making the specific case for legacies.*

Key stage	Media	Strengths and weaknesses
Generating enquiries continued	Cold mail	*Good list*/targeting potential.*
		Likely to be expensive in terms of cost per enquirer, particularly given the need for further investment in follow-up communications to convert enquirers into pledgers.
	Radio advertising	*Small amount of testing but no track record of success as a cost-effective medium for recruiting enquirer.*
	Warm mail	*Speaks to existing supporters who are likely to have a higher propensity to support.*
		Cost effective.
		Allows for intimacy of tone of voice.
		Can be well integrated into a broader communications programme.
	Press ads and inserts in house newsletters and magazines	*Low or zero cost.*
		Well targeted.
		Can combine editorial and direct response disciplines.
Converting enquiries into pledges	Direct mail	*Precisely targeted.*
		Can recognise status of supporter and their previous relationship with the charity.
		Can be through one-off initiatives, such as incentivising[†] pledges, or through on-going contact, such as, for example, a regular legacy-specific newsletter or information sheet.
		Allows for measurable (and initially small-scale) testing of initiatives such as the use of incentives.
Maintaining contact with pledgers	Direct mail	*Can be tailored to individual supporters or types of supporters.*
		Can be through one-off initiatives, such as incentivising pledges, or through ongoing contact, such as a regular legacy-specific newsletter or information sheet.

* A list is literally a list of the names and addresses of prospective supporters, often bought from list brokers, to which is added your own 'house' list.

† 'Giving incentives' or 'incentivising' involves offering items in order to persuade supporters to make a pledge (for example a free book, pen or other item). These items act both as a form of encouragement and an expression of gratitude.

Donor motivations and tone of voice

Any written communication concerning legacy giving, like all fundraising, must be set within the context of proven donor motivations. The list below gives a breakdown of what motivates donors and potential donors to instigate or continue their support of a particular cause.

Of course, all donors are individuals and may have their own specific reasons for giving. It is likely, however, that one or more points from the following list will combine to prompt a donor's financial support.

Do bear in mind that these are not intended as a formal step-by-step checklist, nor are they mutually exclusive. Above all, remember that the final point is the most important!

Why do people give?

- To give something back
- Identification with a cause
- Religious heritage
- Social ambition
- Passionate conviction
- In memoriam
- Guilt
- Ego or self-esteem
- Vested interest (eg in education)
- Self-preservation (eg with cancer or heart disease)
- Recognition or the quest for immortality
- Tax planning
- Because it feels good – people like to give
- Altruism
- Compassion
- Value for money
- Because they were asked.

Whatever communications you produce, try to assess how successfully you have met the donor motivations that are relevant to your own particular target audience.

Integrating legacy fundraising

A key similarity between legacy fundraising and all other forms of fundraising is the need to make a well-articulated case for support. This area, and its relevance to cold and warm audiences, is covered in some detail in Chapter 5. While many fundraisers are well practised and skilled at articulating the need they serve, the proper integration of the legacy case into the wider fundraising mix is often overlooked.

Legacy promotion does not and should not exist in isolation but, unfortunately for many charities, it has done so in the past. Indeed, when pro-active legacy promotion began, it was often added on to the legacy administration function rather than seen as a marketing or direct-marketing role. Legacy promotion through direct marketing is in fact an enormously wide discipline and must be integrated seamlessly into the wider fundraising mix. What precisely does this entail?

Integration means primarily ensuring that, from the donor's perspective, your organisation speaks with one voice. This means ensuring that a volunteer involved in face-to-face fundraising makes the same key points as those portrayed in your legacy information leaflet. It means ensuring that your legacy promotion mailing does not arrive on the doormat on the same day as your membership magazine. It means ensuring that the activities of regional groups or branches work with, and not across, initiatives that originate from 'head office'. This all requires meticulous strategic planning, as well as consistent creative briefing, and detailed campaign analysis.

Opening the relationship

Various forms of printed material have played an important role in many successful legacy promotion campaigns. Here a number of tangible examples are examined to demonstrate the importance of reader friendliness, clear messages, publications with a strategic role and integration.

In the late 1980s and early 1990s several charities began to adopt a structured, measurable approach to promoting legacies via direct marketing. Their motivation was clear: to develop an accountable strategy to secure and build on what had previously been windfall income – unexpected, unpredictable but exceptionally welcome. Many causes rightly saw a danger in relying for core funding on an unmanaged source of income.

It is generally recognised that the WorldWide Fund for Nature (WWF), the Young Men's Christian Association (YMCA) and the Royal National Institute for the Blind (RNIB) were among the first causes to go down the 'legacy information' route. This involved using a booklet on 'How to make or change your will' as a hook to generate interest and enquiries from the general public with a view to then converting these enquiries into pledges.

CASE STUDY RNIB

RNIB used celebrity-based advertisements to generate initial interest. A detailed programme of testing allowed the charity to evaluate which creative treatments and which media were the most cost-effective channels for generating enquiries. So, for example, a 'Read the large print' advertisement could be tested against a 'Solve the mystery of making a will' treatment in a range of national newspapers and lifestyle magazines (see Figures 10.1 and 10.2). This form of testing and tracking of response via reply codes allows for a gradually evolving programme which remains entirely accountable in terms of expenditure.

Figure 10.1 Legacy advertisement: RNIB

Figure 10.2 Legacy advertisement: RNIB

These advertisements follow the classic Attention, Interest, Desire, Action framework. The more successful of the two was the Miss Marples celebrity ad (Figure 10.2), where a famous face with an appropriate 'mystery' headline is used to attract attention. Importantly, this is not just any celebrity, but one who is similar in profile to the target audience. The murder-mystery-scenario copy is intriguing and carries the reader to the reply coupon, where the offer of free information is made. Here again, the target audience is carefully considered so that the information booklet is offered in four formats: standard print, large print, tape cassette and Braille. This reinforces part of RNIB's core mission – to improve accessibility of information – as well as broadening the offer to include as many people as possible. A key lesson for fundraisers lies in the large proportion of responders requesting large print.

Providing information in various formats will clearly have a cost implication. This applies not simply at this initial stage, but throughout the future relationship with responders. While this can be onerous, it is liable to bear fruit in the long term by positioning the charity as truly supporter friendly.

Creative executions for radio advertising that develop the treatment of successful legacy press advertising have been tested, most notably on stations such as Classic FM. It is fair to say, however, that radio has not yet proved itself able to compete with the low costs per enquirer and costs per pledge that result from both press advertising to the general public and, increasingly, direct mail cultivation to existing supporters.

When buying media space for such advertising there will always be some discount available against the rate-card price quoted by the advertising sales team. Discounts of some size are generally available to charities. Space sold late at so-called 'distress rates' is particularly cost effective but often demands quick turnaround of artwork.

In addition to the choice of publications to advertise in, an important consideration is your charity's position within the publication. The crucial advice here is 'Don't compromise!' An advertisement tucked away in the inner margin of the latter half of a paper will perform substantially less well than one on a prominent outside edge of an earlier page.

Of course, advertising can be expensive and may be hard to justify for smaller or medium-sized causes, but your charity's existing publications may offer opportunities to convey the legacy messages. The Royal National Lifeboat Institution (RNLI) has achieved this through advertising, loose inserts and supporting editorial placed in its own magazine, the *Lifeboat*. The following case history illustrates many of the fundamental elements of good legacy promotion.

CASE STUDY RNLI

Key elements of RNLI's campaign were: organisational culture; a letter to establish the need; advertising and loose inserts in the *Lifeboat* ; editorial in the magazine, an authoritative news-format video; and effective PR through TV and radio.

Organisational culture
While this is not primarily a direct-marketing issue, the campaign was strengthened through its origins in an organisation that intuitively values its supporters. Although the campaign of active legacy promotion described below had been in progress since 1995, the organisation has attracted significant levels of legacy income for many years, primarily because of the strong values of courage, selflessness and valour represented by the

volunteer lifeboat crews, coupled with the personal skills and simple courtesy of many staff centrally and in the regions in dealing with donors.

Letter to establish the need

In mid-1995 the Institution discovered that the prognosis for future legacy giving was less than promising. Legacy income had levelled out and threatened to go into decline. For an organisation with a modern life-saving service and 217 lifeboat stations to operate, any decline would be unacceptable and dangerous.

It was therefore decided to write a simple and confidential letter to supporters explaining the potential problem. There was no 'hard sell' and no request for a donation, but simply an intimate letter in which an appropriately serious tone of voice was used for the RNLI to tell its best friends about the issues.

At this stage more than five thousand supporters took the opportunity to let the RNLI know that they had already included the lifeboats in their will. The success of the letter was thus two-fold: first, in bringing the direct reassurance by 'flushing out' already intended legacies; and secondly, in conveying the need to supporters in a responsible, reasonable and serious manner, thereby helping to form the foundation for more focused future initiatives.

Advertising and loose inserts in the *Lifeboat*

The official journal of record for the RNLI is the magazine, the *Lifeboat*. Reaching the key audience of existing RNLI members, it provides the perfect platform for direct-response initiatives such as loose inserts and off-the-page advertising.

The theme of the campaign, and of the legacy booklet, is 'Preserving all you value', the title of the campaign reflecting the organisation's mission – to preserve life at sea – while also appealing to the primarily conservative values of the audience.

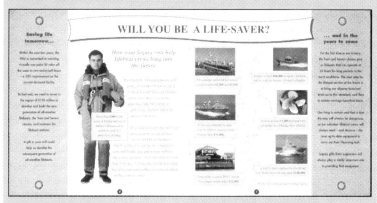

Figure 10.3 Feature in the *Lifeboat*

In contrast to the RNIB campaign, the RNLI campaign includes a more direct means of asking for support. Although a booklet is being offered, it is clear from the first advertisement that the Institution is asking people to include the lifeboat service in their will.

Editorial in the magazine

The journal provides the opportunity to run supporting features that provide an editorial environment favourable to targeted direct-marketing activity. The feature shown here (see Figure 10.3), for example, highlights the vital importance of legacy income in funding the service, gives examples of boats funded in this way, features actual rescues, and makes a direct link to the need: 'three out of every four lifeboat launches and rescues are funded by legacy gifts'. The example demonstrates the direct approach taken in the campaign, and the creative treatments stress the traditional values, heritage and generation-to-generation continuity on which the lifeboat service is founded.

Authoritative news-format video

Several larger causes have produced 'legacy videos' to help promote their cause: these include NSPCC, UNICEF and Marie Curie Cancer Care. The role of such videos is often to break the ice within local and regional meetings at which the topic of legacies is to be discussed. Many fundraisers are reticent or inhibited about the issue and find that the authority of an independent on-screen message introduces the subject smoothly and sensitively.

With all such promotion the style and tone of voice are vital. Anything too gimmicky or irreverent stands a real chance of alienating the predominantly older target audience. RNLI's video used the format of a news programme, fronted by Michael Buerk, to present the launch of the legacy campaign with authority and seriousness (see Figure 10.4).

Media coverage through TV and radio

All regional television stations will be interested in a strong human-interest story, particularly one that can be presented with visual drama. The RNLI capitalised on this by issuing to the regional news stations a video 'news release' of edited highlights of the legacy video. One of these stations, News South East, sent along a film crew to interview the RNLI's head of fundraising and marketing as well as interviewing two pledgers who featured in the booklet.

The level of coverage generated – about three minutes on screen in a prime-time news slot, broadcast to the retirement communities of the south coast – was priceless to the RNLI and demonstrates that free, high-profile news space is available to organisations that can present themselves in a news-friendly manner.

Figure 10.4 Cover of RNLI legacy video

Developing enquirers

Once potential legators have made contact with a charity, and become 'enquirers', they need to be cultivated. For RNIB this is done via a special 'legacy newsletter' called *Foresight*. The newsletter builds on the enquirer's initial interest to give them more information about the cause, to keep them abreast of changes in the law and, crucially, to maintain a long-term dialogue with them. Why is this crucial? Primarily because people change as time goes by.

It is not unusual for a legacy enquiry to be converted to a pledge long after the initial enquiry. This should not surprise us, as making a will is undoubtedly one of the most-delayed activities any of us ever undertake. Good intentions are overtaken by more immediate concerns, personal circumstances change – there is almost always something more pressing to do. It is therefore vital for a charity to keep the legacy message in front of supporters so that it stands as good a chance as possible of being at the front of a person's mind when the time comes to make or change their will. RNIB has found that each edition of the newsletter brought in a fresh batch of legacy pledges.

Over the past few years, the environment within which fundraisers operate has changed radically. Older people are faced with having to fund their own care in a way that would have been unheard of ten years ago. Some legacy fundraisers see this added financial burden as a contributory factor to a bleak outlook for legacy income. More optimistic fundraisers see that, as people are increasingly forced to tackle the issue of financial planning, there is scope for engaging donors in a way that they would previously have found inappropriate or uncomfortable.

Figure 10.5 Front cover of *Botton Village Life*: legacies *can* be headline news!

One spin-off of this change in climate is a greater directness in the way in which support is asked for by legacy fundraisers. The campaign run by the RNLI shows that it is possible to raise the subject in a direct, sensitive and responsible manner. Of course, the RNLI is a large organisation which already receives huge legacy income. Despite the organisation's unique position, however, the principles of its legacy communication programme outlined above will apply to small, medium and large organisations.

Certainly some of the principles of cost-effective use of existing materials will apply to all kinds of organisations and vehicles, such as newsletters, magazines and annual reports. The example of the Botton Village* newsletter, *Botton Village Life*, shows how the sensitive topic of legacies can be portrayed as a 'news item' for supporters (see Figure 10.5). This sends some important implicit messages to supporters:

- it is possible to support the cause in this way;
- the support makes an important contribution to the cause;
- people like you do it already!

How to make your materials reader-friendly

Readability is a crucial issue for fundraisers generally and for legacy fundraisers in particular. You will often be communicating with readers who are middle aged or older, and who are less visually literate (in graphic design terms) than their juniors. So, while this is not an audience to be patronised, it is an audience that will welcome your efforts to be reader friendly.

TOPIC SUMMARY MORE EFFECTIVE PRINT COMMUNICATION

1 Remember that no one *has* to read your communication. The communication should work hard to attract and maintain attention.

2 Legacy publications don't need to be dull! Make the most of the drama or human interest of your cause.

3 Most of your readers will be 50 years old or more, and their eyesight will be deteriorating. You need therefore to set your type at a decent size. Take a look at older, 'lifestyle' publications for tips on design and layout.

4 Make sure that your designer has read your text and fully understands the needs of your target audience.

---

* Botton Village is part of the Camphill Village Trust, a charity that sets up communities in which people with learning disabilities live and work in extended families.

5 Make sure that your designer understands the key principles of readability, including use of headlines, colour, backgrounds and tints, justification, reversed type, typefaces, styles and sizes, and the importance of reading gravity (this is a term to describe the way in which the eye moves across a page of text – top left to bottom right is the basic and most comfortable movement, but there are ways of capturing attention as the eye sweeps across the page).

6 Use only good quality photographs. A poor photograph is *not* better than none at all!

7 Use 'involvement devices' such as questions, surveys and so on.

8 Ensure that staff are properly trained in how to use your publications.

9 Have an elderly relative look at your materials. If they find them reader unfriendly, so will your donors.

10 Be prepared to break any of the above rules *if you have a good reason to.*

The Internet

The Internet may not yet be the answer to every fundraiser's prayers but it is already being used in the USA, where the target audience is known as 'CyberSeniors'*. These are people who are linked up to the Worldwide Web and who use it for all kinds of everyday financial transaction and product research. This activity includes their financial planning, which undoubtedly links into potential legacy giving.

In general, CyberSeniors use the Internet to:

- stay in touch with family (especially grandchildren) via e-mail;
- explore travel opportunities;
- manage their finances;
- follow their stock portfolios;
- obtain health information.

A 1995 survey of Americans aged 55 or over showed that:

- 29 per cent owned a personal computer (an increase of 21 per cent in 16 months);
- 32 per cent of 65–74 year olds own personal computers;
- 23 per cent of over-75 year olds owned personal computers;
- 28 per cent of computer owners regularly used an on-line service;
- 65 per cent of on-line users had accessed the Internet in the past month.

* For all the information in this section many thanks to Natasha van Bentum at Greenpeace Canada.

People interested in looking at the world of CyberSeniors can start at:

http://www.senior.com *or*

http://www.retireweb.com

Monitoring, tracking and evaluation

With all forms of direct marketing, it is essential to monitor the effectiveness of any money you spend. This is an important and varied discipline. It is important because you may be investing substantial amounts in a campaign and, as with all forms of fundraising, you will need to assess accurately the return on your investment. It is varied because the level of monitoring and assessment you will need to carry out may begin with looking at response to an individual advertisement, whereas in the longer term you will be able to plot actual income from the types of legacy that result from the various forms of recruitment and development media and campaigns you have carried out.

Such tracking and assessment must be done on the basis of meticulous record keeping. This is particularly vital given the long-term nature of legacy promotion. There is a strong chance that a legacy campaign will last a good deal longer than the time a legacy fundraiser stays in post, and there is certainly every chance that a legacy fundraiser will move to another post within their organisation, or indeed move to another organisation after a couple of years or so. A legacy fundraiser's key bequest, therefore, will be the legacy of information left for his or her successor. While the monitoring and evaluation process can be infinitely varied, the following gives a simplified guide to essential core information:

- date
- campaign description
- source code
- quantity mailed
- total number of enquiries
- percentage response rate
- cost per enquiry
- total number of pledges
- rate of conversion (enquirers to pledgers)
- cost of pledge
- rate of conversion (pledges and legacies)

- income value

- total cost.

Such monitoring and tracking will in the long term allow you to assess the levels and types of legacy gift that are generated by a particular campaign. You will be able to track back to see the effectiveness of various sources of recruitment and varying development strategies used to build a fruitful dialogue with potential legacy givers.

Clearly, within the above structure you will want absolute detail of each individual campaign: which titles perform best for you, which creative approaches, which audience segments, which times of year, and so on.

Importantly, any spreadsheet information should be accompanied by annotations describing the broader environment within which your campaign was taking place. External factors, such as a General Election for example, can all have an effect on the mood of the country and thereby indirectly affect the results of a particular campaign.

Acknowledgements

Thanks are due in particular to David Brann and colleagues at the RNLI for permission to share a good part of RNLI's experience in this field. Thanks also to Natasha van Bentum and Valerie Morton, RNIB.

CHAPTER ELEVEN

Telephone contact

Sebastian Wilberforce

The use of the telephone in legacy fundraising is relatively recent, and techniques for its use are still being refined. One lesson that seems to be emerging is the need to follow up a pledge given over the telephone with a request for written confirmation of intent. (It is very easy to get rid of a caller by giving them the information they want.) This chapter describes how to use the telephone on an *ad hoc* or reactive basis, or systematically as a pro-active campaign tool.

Introduction

The previous chapter proceeded from the need to integrate direct marketing legacy promotion into the wider fundraising mix. The same approach applies to the use of the telephone. At what stage of a fundraising campaign can you use the telephone to secure legacy pledges? What information can you secure on direct marketing response devices (or from correspondence) for planning or undertaking telephone campaigns?

Thinking through your responses to questions such as these will help you select those to work with by telephone. Planning ahead can also make conversations more fruitful for both the prospect and the caller.

Such advance information might consist of:

- factors relevant to the will-making process, such as the stage prospects are at, their family circumstances, whether they have a solicitor, what technical knowledge they require to help them move along;
- estimated or actual age of the prospect;
- their knowledge of or interest in your cause;

- whether they wish to leave, or have already left, a legacy to your cause (and if so why?);
- what further communication the contact wants with your charity, and by what means.

(See Chapters 6 and 7 of this volume for further discussion of research and profiling to secure the above information.)

Unique characteristics of legacy fundraising calling

- Legacy telephoning is intensive, and time consuming. Only 15–18 calls can be made in an evening between 6 and 9 pm (as opposed to 26–30 calls in other campaigns).
- Making a legacy pledge is a longer-term decision than deciding to make an immediate donation, so tracking results is more difficult.
- Agency conversations can average 15–20 minutes each (remember that the call is likely to be the first personal contact with your organisation that a prospect has had), and in-house ones (where there is detailed knowledge of the cause) are often considerably longer.
- There is more dialogue than in a general fundraising call.
- Discussion of legacy donations is intensely personal; this means that telephone contact can be very rewarding, presenting an ideal means by which to establish the actual or potential warmth of individuals to your cause, their stage in the will-making process, and move them on to pledging a legacy and making a will.
- Telephone contact is a valuable market research tool, providing feedback, for instance, on your marketing materials and on motivations to pledge.
- Before you embark on legacy fundraising calling, you will need to consider whether your charity has the resources to sustain the use of the telephone for this purpose: once prospects are familiar with telephone contact, they may come to expect it, and, for the reasons given above, this is not a cheap option.
- The use of the telephone in legacy fundraising is a fast-developing tool. It is proving effective, and an increasing number of organisations are trying it.

Targets for telephone contact

Possible targets for telephone contact include supporters on your charity's donor database (warm prospects), enquirers for either your will-making pack (cold prospects) or your legacy leaflet (possible pledgers), and perhaps intermediaries such as solicitors.

Making calls (out-bound usage)

Calls can be made by a charity or a telephone fundraising agency operating on its behalf, either as part of a one-off legacy fundraising campaign or as an ongoing activity (see below). As part of a legacy campaign, the call could follow up a mailing specifically asking for legacies, or a will pack requested by an enquirer.

The aim of out-bound calls is directly to secure pledges, or to move prospects, or intending or possible pledgers, towards pledging. In the course of the phone call it is also important to find out, or to provide, such information as may be required to help either with making the decision to pledge, or to support a particular aspect of your charity's work, or to do with will-making itself, in order to move the pledger along.

Other aims of telephone use might be to update the information you hold on your enquirers, to do research with prospects or pledgers, to establish a databank of friendly solicitors or to maintain contact with them. Also, of course, it can be used to keep pledgers interested in your work.

Receiving calls

There are several advantages in encouraging prospects or pledgers to contact you by telephone:

- expenditure is reduced, since you do not bear the cost of the initial call;
- it is easier to establish what stage in the will-making and pledging process the callers are at, and what information they need;
- it is simpler to open or maintain a dialogue with them;
- you can obtain their telephone number for follow-up work.

During an initial telephone call, you can seek pre-categorised information about a broad range of matters, including what priority the prospect attaches to making a will. This last point is important: it should set the pace of the telephone contact you seek to have with your prospect.

After both initial in-bound and out-bound calls, the charity sends out any further information it has promised to provide. Two to three weeks later (longer if the contact attaches low priority to making a will) the charity can call to check that this has been received, and to find out if any further information is required. This is how the process of warming up prospects to your charity continues, moving them along towards actually making their will. Subsequent calls can be made as necessary.

Once the will has been made, a different communication strategy is required, in which the telephone could also play a part.

Key elements in the use of the telephone in legacy fundraising

Setting objectives

The first consideration is knowing what you want to achieve by calling. (An example of a set of objectives is given below, under 'A stand-alone telephone legacy campaign', page 116.)

Your database is your primary source of contacts. Source codes, recent donor history and giving history, and such information as you can glean through research (for instance, age indicators) will determine not only which numbers to call but how to approach the script and brief the callers. For instance, a regular giver of some years' standing will know more about your organisation than a cold enquirer. What information has the prospect received (in donor mailings, for example) from your organisation over the time they have been on the database? All this information will have a bearing on how the caller conducts a conversation.

A telephone script must not restrict callers, but give them both a path to follow and the freedom to deviate from it as the conversation develops (without ever losing sight of the objectives of the call).

What skills does the caller team require?

Fundraisers carrying out telephone work need listening skills, sensitivity and intuition. It is important to be aware of what a prospect is saying to the caller, both directly and indirectly, and to read the situation as the call progresses. For instance, is the prospect expressing reservations about some aspect of your charity, or is he or she worried about being able to afford a legacy?

The caller must aim both to understand the prospect and also to make the call work for the charity. Ultimately, this means not making prospects feel uncomfortable if they are *not* doing what they are being asked to do. You want them to feel good about your charity, whether they are giving it a legacy or not. They may be able to help in other ways (such as making a donation) or just by helping create, or increase, positive awareness among friends and family. A legacy might be written into their wills at a later date.

The caller should listen out for unsolicited information that may give pointers on how (or when) the request for a legacy should be made (or repeated). This kind of information also gives something away about prospects' circumstances, which may suggest why they are (or are not) supporting your charity; it may also be relevant to the way in which you build a relationship with them (eg their interests, and what family members they have).

Legacy fundraising callers should always be fully briefed on:

- the charity and its work: often the caller is seen as the charity; empathy with the charity's aims is important, and a caller's warmth of expression (as long as this is not overdone) and commitment may be infectious;
- the people being contacted, with as much detail about individuals as is available;
- the technicalities of will making – basic advice is all that is needed; callers must appreciate the limitations of their own knowledge and be honest about more detailed questions they are unable to answer; they should have the name and number of someone (such as the charity's legacy administrator) who can give more information – better still, they could make a note and tell the prospect that the appropriate person will call them back, and when.

The timing of calls

Calls are often made too late after the prospect has received a will-making pack or a printed request for a legacy. If the telephone is being used to follow up such materials, calls should ideally be made two to three weeks after the materials are delivered.

Telephone contact is not only useful for a dedicated campaign: it is also a valuable tool on an *ad hoc* basis. If someone writes in for information about will making or leaving a legacy, you can give them a ring, or follow up a letter with a call. The objectives of the calls are the same as in other legacy telephone use, but be prepared for lengthy conversations (calls lasting 45 minutes are not unusual).

A stand-alone telephone legacy campaign

Setting objectives

These might be:

- to contact people who have requested your will pack;
- to offer (and provide) additional information, to move them on to deciding whether or not to support your cause in their will (if they have not done so), and to help them make the will;
- to ask people to confirm their pledge in writing, by means of returning a pledge form;
- to clean up the database;
- to obtain feedback about your legacy marketing materials.

Specific targets, which can later be evaluated, should also be set at the outset of a campaign. These could include:

- conversion rates;
- call quality and complaint rates;
- return on investment;
- qualitative analysis of responses.

Selecting prospects

Two criteria are usually used to select prospects: *age* and *warmth*. As far as age is concerned, it makes sense to target those whose pledges are likely to yield sooner rather than later. The usual indicators, or evidence, of age can be applied: postcode, first name, handwriting, voice (if you've spoken to them on the telephone before), date of birth (if you've asked for it) or source code (if recruited through advertising in 'grey' media, for example).

Warmth of prospects is often measured by reference to their giving history, since this is frequently all that can be afforded by way of database analysis. Generally, charity members are the most responsive, followed by committed givers, donors and cold prospects in that order. What hard records have you got? Do they yield indicators (for example, a response declining, with regret, an invitation to an event) that might suggest interest in, or commitment to, your charity?

Pre-call letter

Because the process of requesting a legacy is so sensitive, it is advisable to write before telephoning. Give your prospects the chance to opt out of being called (they may have already left a legacy or have recently been bereaved), to tell you that they are going away, or to prepare any questions about the technicalities of will making or about your cause. A pre-call letter provides a means of warming people up to the request, and of dismissing those who respond badly to the telephone. Opt-out rates are low, usually only 2–5 per cent.

The letter should:

- thank the prospects for their interest;
- underline the importance of making a will;
- give some information about your cause and the importance of legacy income;
- mention the call, and give the prospects the chance to opt out of being called.

The letter should be sent two weeks before calls start and should not include a response device.

The script

More flexibility has to be built into a script for legacy telephoning than for general fundraising calls, which more easily allow for an immediate 'yes' or 'no' answer. A legacy call is more of a conversation and a negotiation, given the other potential demands on the prospect's assets and the potential size of the gift. As a result, a legacy fundraising telephone script is more general and vague about the charity than that for general fundraising calls, focusing less on the day-to-day workings of the charity and more on the future and the vision. The script must, of course, ensure that the objectives of the exercise are attained, but it must be structured in such a way as to allow several different pathways to this end (see Figure 11.1). The script must also invite prospects to be pro-active in the information they require about the charity, which is especially where flexibility in the script and the caller's knowledge of the cause come in.

If the prospect knows less about your organisation than you thought, or has an interest in one particular aspect of your work, then you can steer the conversation accordingly, perhaps by means of a script of bullet points. More closely scripted responses are needed for legal technicalities unless the caller has a sound knowledge of these.

A script approach

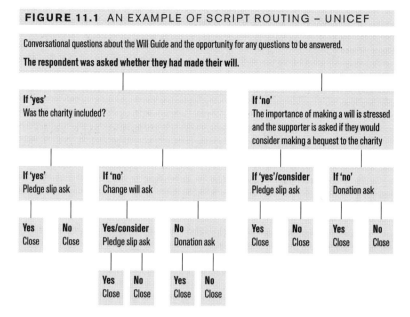

FIGURE 11.1 AN EXAMPLE OF SCRIPT ROUTING – UNICEF

Conversational questions about the Will Guide and the opportunity for any questions to be answered.
The respondent was asked whether they had made their will.

If 'yes'
Was the charity included?

If 'no'
The importance of making a will is stressed and the supporter is asked if they would consider making a bequest to the charity

If 'yes'
Pledge slip ask

If 'no'
Change will ask

If 'yes'/consider
Pledge slip ask

If 'no'
Donation ask

Yes
Close

No
Close

Yes/consider
Pledge slip ask

No
Donation ask

Yes
Close

No
Close

Yes
Close

No
Close

Yes
Close

No
Close

Yes
Close

No
Close

- The script opened with an attempt to find out whether the contact had found the information sent useful and informative and whether the contact had made a will since receiving the pack.

- Depending on the reply to this question, the script then moved on to a request to:
  return a pledge form – if the contact had already made a bequest to UNICEF;
  consider changing the will so as to include UNICEF – if he or she had already made a will;
  consider UNICEF when making a will – if the contact had not already done so.

- A special promotion was presented as a reason why 'now was such a good time' to make a will. The data was broken down into regional groups in order to be able to offer information on the nearest solicitor.

- A conscious decision was made not to mention much about UNICEF's work, as it was felt that contacts would be well enough informed at this stage.

- As a final default, the contact was asked for a small donation.

The script should contain default requests: perhaps a request for a donation if a refusal to pledge is given, or a request to follow up the conversation at a later date if, for instance, the prospect cannot consider pledging at the moment or wants to delay making a will.

Tracing telephone numbers

With the increasing use of ex-directory lines, the Telephone Preference Service* and the use of telecommunication services other than BT's, it is becoming more and more difficult to trace numbers. In the long term, requests on response devices for telephone numbers will help.

There are tracing agencies specialising in the charity sector. They work by taking your data disk and matching the addresses and postcodes on it against BT's standard directory.

The timing of calls

The decision on when to call is linked to your decision about whom to call first. You need to develop a means of identifying what priority your prospects attach to making a will, linked to how warm they are to your cause. Obviously, the higher the priority attached to making a will and the greater the degree of warmth to the cause, the sooner the call should be made. Calls should be placed as soon as two weeks after a mailing, to be sure of catching those people who intend to make a will without delay. Include in the mailing some text that can act as a pre-call letter. Follow-up calls to those who attach less priority to the task can be put in your diary.

Call sheets

Information gained from telephone calls should always be recorded immediately on call sheets. Data can be entered on to a database.

The call sheets should be kept to inform future telephone or even face-to-face work. Some soft information is likely to be recorded that cannot be included in the database but that can yield useful information for both research and evaluation when call sheets are analysed.

* Telephone Preference Service: Haymarket House, 1 Oxenden Street, London, SW1V 4EE. Tel: 0171 766 4420.

Fulfilment

Some prospects may make a pledge over the telephone, but on reflection may give more consideration to other people and organisations they could leave their estate to. Getting written confirmation of the pledge is a valuable indicator of a pledger's seriousness of intent. Applying the principle that response should be made as easy as possible, mail a simple A4 letter with a tear-off slip to be returned in a reply envelope. The tear-off slip can seek to elicit the type of legacy, and such other information as there is space for.

Given the importance of getting a response, it is unwise to dilute the impact of this letter with too many other materials. These could even follow in a separate (subsequent or previous) mailing.

Experience shows that response rates to letters asking pledgers to provide written confirmation of their pledge are usually promising. For one charity, 82 per cent of those who had said they would leave a legacy returned the tear-off slip from the bottom of a one-page letter asking them to confirm this pledge which was sent to them the day after the call. It has also been found that 60 per cent of pledge forms give the value of their bequest if this is requested.

Fulfilment also presents an opportunity for the charity to ask if there is anything else it can do for the supporter, thereby maintaining a dialogue and cementing a relationship.

If a pledge form is not returned within, say, six weeks of its despatch to the prospect, a reminder call could be placed, or a reminder mailing sent.

Evaluating a campaign

Evaluation of legacy campaigns is an imprecise science because of the nature of will making and legacies. Some prospects take over a year to get down to making their will: telephoning them regularly to move them along is insensitive and can be counter-productive. It is also not always possible to quantify the value of pledges: not all pledgers will disclose the fact, and the size of residuary bequests cannot be calculated in advance.

Evaluation can usually be made against specific targets chosen at the onset of the campaign (see 'Setting objectives', above). Conversion rates depend on the warmth of the prospect to the organisation, and vary from one organisation to the next. Response rates of 4 per cent from warm prospects and 2 per cent from cold are not unusual, although recently a rate of nearer 8 per cent from warm has been achieved. Response rates to use of the telephone comfortably exceed mailing response rates. (See the case study on pp 122–23 on a legacy telemarketing campaign by Shelter for two ways of presenting this information.)

Feedback on telephone fundraising is important: it helps determine whether the pitch of the campaign was right, and can provide other research information. Evaluation also informs follow-up work and sets parameters against which future telephone campaigns may be measured.

In-house or agency?

Telephone campaigns can be conducted by in-house staff or by a specialised agency. Key factors which will determine which to use are:

- availability of experienced and knowledgeable callers, and time to train them;
- suitable technology to heighten quality of calling, speed of fulfilment and data analysis;
- good facilities with individual booths to reduce background noise;
- trained managers capable of dealing with problems.

An advantage of agencies is that they can give you the benefit of their experience with other charities.

The ICFM Code of Practice on out-bound telephone fundraising

Before beginning telephone work, obtain a copy of the Code of Practice direct from ICFM (see p 185). The code covers work by a charity, or by an external agency, and includes:

- the telephone briefing process;
- payment of telephone operators;
- content and communication of the request for support;
- use of a pre-call letter and of a script;
- information to be disclosed to the prospect;
- the tone of calls;
- complaints procedure;
- the legal prohibition of calls after 9 pm;
- people who should not or do not want to be called.

Do not skip the footnotes to the code: they cover important matters such as the Charities Act 1992 and data protection requirements.

In this telemarketing campaign, 1,118 prospects were rung up and asked the question 'Will you leave Shelter a legacy?' Following the phone call, those who had either promised to leave a legacy or said they might (when they made the decision to leave a legacy at all) were sent a letter that sought to secure written confirmation of their decision to pledge. The results of the campaign are given in Tables 11.1 and 11.2.

TABLE 11.1 RESPONSE TO THE QUESTION 'WILL YOU LEAVE SHELTER A LEGACY?', BROKEN DOWN BY SUPPORTER TYPE

	Yes	Possible	No	Donation	Total
Donors					315
Pledged	13	86	–	17	116
Response*	14	16	16	31	77
Conversion	107.7%	18.6%	–	182.3%	66.4%
Segment response rate (n=315)	4.4%	5%	5%	9.8%	24.4%
Overall response rate (n=1,118)	1.3%	1.4%	1.4%	2.8%	6.8%
Regular givers					75
Pledged	8	41	–	0	49
Response*	6	6	4	3	19
Conversion	75%	14.6%	–	–	38.7%
Segment response rate (n=75)	8%	8%	5.3%	4%	25.3%
Overall response rate (n=1,118)	0.5%	0.5%	0.4%	0.3%	1.7%
Enquirers					728
Pledged	18	204	–	13	235
Response*	9	9	82	9	109
Conversion	50%	4.4%	–	69.2%	46.4%
Segment response rate (n=728)	1.2%	1.2%	11.3%	1.2%	15.0%
Overall response rate (n=1,118)	0.8%	0.8%	7.3%	0.8%	9.7%

* Response indicates those pledgers, or possible pledgers, who replied to a follow-up letter in which Shelter asked for written confirmation of the decision they had announced on the phone.

TABLE 11.2 OVERALL RESPONSE TO THE QUESTION 'WILL YOU LEAVE SHELTER A LEGACY?', MEASURED AGAINST PLEDGE (N = 1,118)

	Yes	Possibly	No	Donation	Total
Pledged	39	331	–	30	400
Response*	32	33	114	43	222
Conversion	82.1%	10.0%	–	143.3%	55.5%
Overall response rate (n=1,118)					
	2.9%	3.0%	10.1%	3.8%	19.9%

* Response indicates those pledgers, or possible pledgers, who replied to a follow-up letter in which Shelter asked for written confirmation of the decision they had announced on the phone.

A donor's perspective 4

I don't really understand why so many charities have to keep on talking to me about wills and things. Like everyone I give my support as I can and that's what it's about really. Yes, I have got a will, but that's my business and I think that once I'm dead what is important to me is private – I don't really want to discuss it with you even now and I certainly don't want to discuss it with charities that I have never heard of before and with whom I don't have any particular interest. In fact, the more information I get from any of these charities, the less I'm inclined to give them my support even now, let alone when I'm dead.

Yes, I do have a covenant with the church and with a couple of other charities – one of which I have been involved with for over ten years now, but that's how I give my support and I'm not very interested in doing it in any other way.

Yes, I know legacies are an important source of income to charities. Someone said to me once that they are one of the largest sources of support. But that's not the point from my point of view. My will is made, and that's it. No, I don't think I will amend my will in favour of any charity, even the ones that I support now, because I don't see that it is relevant.

CHAPTER TWELVE

Face-to-face contact

Sebastian Wilberforce

There is a technique to face-to-face fundraising, which involves setting your objectives before the meeting, managing the conversation during it so as the better to achieve them, deducing the sort of person you are dealing with and acting accordingly, and asking open, rather than closed, questions. Once mastered, face-to-face fundraising is a remarkably effective medium and also, on the whole, very enjoyable.

The value of face-to-face work

One-to-one work, in person, is a golden opportunity to get the prospect fully behind what your organisation seeks to achieve. For that person, you are the face of the charity and quite possibly will remain so. How you appear and what you say will send all sorts of signals to the prospect about the professionalism and dedication of the charity to its work – even if you are a fundraiser and not actually a service provider or campaigner! How you do your job will be taken as an indicator of how the rest of the organisation performs. Your presence may well secure the gift.

Meeting face to face can provide all sorts of information about prospects, including their wealth and personal circumstances. In a face-to-face interview, you can:

- establish what motivates the prospect (see Table 12.1);
- have a full dialogue;
- identify and meet the prospect's need for information;
- enthuse them about your cause;
- take them through the range of legacy options;
- explain what would most help you;
- perhaps seek to increase the size of their legacy;

- find out why this person is interested in your organisation;
- establish the basis for your future relationship with the pledger.

The knowledge obtained informs your relationship with that individual and helps secure the most appropriate legacy from them. It can also provide market research for your legacy fundraising generally.

TABLE 12.1 ASSESSING THE TYPE OF LEGATOR

Type of legator	Motivation
Community lovers	Desire to help community
Devout	Compelled by religious beliefs
Investors	Looking to the future
Socialites	Giving decisions based on social environment
Repayers	Sense of fulfilling a perceived obligation (often users or relatives of users)
Altruists	Means of self-fulfilment with philanthropic overtones
Traditionalists	Giving is function of family history or tradition

Source Richard Radcliffe, Smee & Ford.

How to choose which prospects to see

Face-to-face work takes up a lot of time so you will probably need to give a priority to the prospects you intend to see. Bearing in mind that a legacy is purely a vehicle for supporting the work of your organisation, focus on those who are warmest to it. Face-to-face work *can* be done with cold prospects, but only over a longer term, given the need to warm them up.

Again, integration of fundraising activity reaps rewards. Some charities use responses to mailings to identify which prospects to see. They focus first on those who have indicated that they intend to leave a legacy or are considering doing so, but they will also approach donors to suggest this type of gift.

Shuffle the pile of prospects' details you have, so as to determine the order in which they might be approached and visited. You will always apply pre-set criteria to this process, using factors such as:

- known will-making intentions;
- area or region (analysis of your legators may indicate that some regions yield more legacies than others);

- age (which can be indicated, if it is not known, by first name, handwriting or even information you've asked for);
- family status (focusing on spinsters, bachelors, widows or widowers, for example);
- residential address (for instance, a house name rather than a street number; certain postcodes).

Meeting intending or possible pledgers

There are many ways to secure meetings in person with possible pledgers. You could, for example, offer to see them to advise them on how to make their wills, to thank them for their support or to tell them more about your charity's work. With donors who haven't received or responded to a mailed request for a legacy, you might tell them that you are going to be in their area over a particular period and ask to see them to deliver some literature, to tell them more about your work or to bring them up to date. A request for a legacy can be worked into the course of your subsequent conversation.

Other indirect methods for securing meetings might involve:

- giving talks into which a legacy proposition is worked, together with the offer of one-to-one advice;
- the use of a video or cassette as a warm-up device in a mailing;
- talking to volunteer fundraisers about wills and legacies with the stated aim of informing them about propositions to put to supporters, the sub-text being 'you could give in this way too';
- working legacy propositions into other events such as tours of establishments.

How to secure legacy pledges face to face

Before your meeting

- Establish what you already know about the prospect, most importantly how warm they are to your cause and what previous contact they have had with it. Any other information you have will be useful too.
- Is there anything you should send them that will set the scene? For instance, one legacy fundraiser always sends a copy of the charity's will-making booklet in advance of a face-to-face meeting majoring on will advice; the booklet, of course, contains a request for a legacy.
- Set your objectives for the meeting.

- Rehearse what a legacy can achieve and double check that you know the key facts about your organisation and its work.
- Identify the materials to take to give to your prospect.

The meeting

The key is to listen, to observe and to be patient. From the moment you arrive at the property, use your eyes and ears: any information you pick up may give an indication of the prospect's motivation and ability to pledge (and to what extent) and will help you conduct a conversation with them and determine the best approach to adopt for the request.

Begin the meeting by putting the prospect at ease, building up their trust in you and perhaps taking prompts from what you see around you to get them talking about themselves. Consider injecting humour into the conversation if appropriate, so that their encounter with you may be enjoyable and memorable. Listen to what the prospect tells you about themselves. Some facts may inform your approach to the way in which you make your request. One pledger complained of the isolation she experienced through being a wheelchair user: the fundraiser was able to tell her later of the isolation experienced so often by blind people (his client group), knowing that she could relate to that.

If the prospect is a donor, ask them why they support your organisation. Steer the conversation around to your organisation and its work. Have you been able to glean any pointers to aspects that might interest the prospect? If so, these should inform the approach you take. Don't give a monologue, but try to talk in a way that leads to questions. Be informed, and show your commitment. The authority with which you speak, and your conviction, should speak volumes.

Observe the prospect's reaction (including their body language), to gauge the level of interest and comprehension. Does this particular prospect want detailed analysis, for instance? Speak in their language (see Table 12.2). Should you be focusing on what journalists call 'human interest' stories? Can you relate your organisation's work to the prospect's own experience? Can you identify some aspect of your work where they would feel that their support would make a difference? Always go softly: never lecture, nor use emotional blackmail. Listen out for negative language that might suggest a lack of enthusiasm, particularly if they have supported your organisation before. You will need to address this.

TABLE 12.2 SENSORY-SPECIFIC LANGUAGE

Type of person	Type of language used	Communication and attitudes to adopt
Auditory person	That sounds good. I hear what you're saying. That rings a bell.	*Phone and mail – might want to keep a distance. Use of language. Ask, in writing, about the feasibility of a legacy and what the next step should be.*
Feeling person	That feels right. I was moved by what you say. That made an impact.	*Face to face, emotional, instinctive, so might want a project visit. Ask what their feelings are about leaving a legacy.*
Visual person	I get the picture. It's clear now. I see what you mean.	*Face to face or video – will want to see project. Pictures and photos wanted. Create a picture of what they might achieve by their legacy.*

Source Richard Radcliffe, Smee & Ford.

Making the request

When you have given what you think is the right amount of information, you should make your request, in the words of Pat Wise from NSPCC, 'gently and sideways'. One of two different approaches could be used (rehearse your approach before the meeting).

1 If you are giving advice on will making, work your request into that. Take the prospect through the matters their will should cover one by one, including charitable legacies; drop humour in, gently. When discussing funeral wishes, for instance, you could mention the man who directed that his ashes be scattered among the roses in the local park, so his dog could pay its respects each morning in the usual way. More often than not the mere mention of charitable legacies will be sufficient for you to be told that your cause will appear. Take the prospect through the legacy options and don't forget to make sure, in your relief at having secured a pledge, that you have covered everything else that should be in a will. However, if you know enough to be able to give only outline advice, stick to that: the prospect's solicitor can fill in the details.

2 Thank them for their previous support and ask why it was given. Expand on your services and achievements, and talk generally about your organisation's financial needs, perhaps focusing on the cost of one particular activity. (If you do this, make sure that the activity is sufficiently expensive to make the prospect think in terms of legacy-sized gifts and not donor-appeal-sized ones.) Bring the conversation round to how those needs are (or could be) met. Move on to legacies with an opening gambit such as 'Legacies are very, very important. You know, recently, we had one for £X,000 from Mr Bloggs.' Explain

how it was used and why he gave or might have given. Ask if your prospect might consider helping in that way too, and find out what information they need to make a decision or to put the gift in their will. Use open questions rather than closed ones: 'How do you feel about giving a legacy to X?' rather than 'Will you give a legacy to X?' Open questions leave more scope for negotiation.

Consider asking prospects to think about a residuary gift rather than a pecuniary one. If it seems that the gift in mind is a modest pecuniary, a technique for upgrading it is to ask the prospect to think about what one pound would have bought twenty-five years ago and what it will buy now. Older people, particularly, can lose track of the value of money over time, and this is a good way of getting them to think more realistically about the needs of your organisation.

If your request for a legacy is refused, ask why. You may be able to overcome the basis of the refusal.

What makes a good face-to-face legacy fundraiser?

The qualities required of a caller in telephone fundraising (as described in the previous chapter) are also required of a face-to-face fundraiser. Integrity, believability and trustworthiness are crucial, as is empathy. Face-to-face fundraisers hear some very sad and personal stories of woe, and receive confidences: you must care about people and be interested in what makes them tick. A sense of humour and quick wit are very helpful, judiciously used.

Being able to paint a picture in words is valuable, in order to convey (ideally in your prospect's terms) the essence of what it is your charity exists to do. Paint a picture of achievement and hope, a picture your prospect is going to want to buy into.

Sometimes diplomacy and discretion are needed. Fundraisers will talk about witnessing marital and family tensions, or about being told of a serious tax evasion in language that invited endorsement of the activity. One fundraiser met a prospect who had been sacked by his relation (though luckily she didn't realise it). You have to accept individuals' frailties.

As well as listening skills, an understanding of body language is required. Learn how to read the prospect's body language (particularly to identify lack of real interest or failing concentration) and how to ensure yours is open and encouraging.

A crucial final point: you must have enough knowledge of the will-making process to be able to guide people through it, and to remove the inertia that is often engendered by the unfamiliar.

Follow up

In due course, wind up the conversation, having established and agreed what will-making back-up you are to provide; this might include information your pledger wants about your organisation, and an indication of the kind of future contact wanted. Suggest a subsequent meeting. This meeting can be invaluable for re-injecting enthusiasm if you detect that a pledger's commitment has waned since you first met.

Immediately

Write a report on the meeting and make appropriate action points and diary entries. It is advisable to write a letter of thanks, summarising any will-making advice given, thanking again for the pledge and enclosing the wording for a legacy. Is there any case for support literature you could enclose? Your letter will be a useful prompt when the prospect (eventually) gets around to visiting a solicitor. Also, enclose a pledge card and ask the prospect to return it when the will is made.

If yours is a service-providing charity, issues relating to service provision to your prospect may have arisen in the course of your meeting. You need to identify these and pass them on to the appropriate colleague, without getting directly involved yourself (that is not your job). This is not only ethically required, but makes for good relationship building.

Longer term

Not receiving the pledge card is a useful excuse for getting back in touch with prospects. Give them a ring after a month – you've been to their home, after all. Ask them if they've made their will, and whether they have left your charity a legacy: 'I ask because, if you have, you're one of our most generous supporters, and we like to be able to respond to your generosity by keeping you informed about our work and perhaps inviting you to visit us . . . Of course, I quite understand if you regard the contents of your will as private.'

If the prospect has made a pledge, they should be put into your pledger care programme. Your future relationship with them needs to be built on their terms, certainly as regards what future contact is required. Establish what they want (and what it is realistic for you to deliver) at your meeting.

Training for face-to-face fundraisers

Legacy fundraisers working face to face with prospects need the same information as telephone callers:

- a good grounding in your charity's work, the importance of legacy income and its potential impact on that work;
- a sound basic knowledge (at the least) of will making and will changing;
- an understanding of the deterrents to will making, such as lack of knowledge or motivation.

In addition, they need to know:

- the objectives of face-to face-meetings;
- what makes a good face-to-face fundraiser;
- how to conduct a face-to-face meeting, in terms of conversation and recording information;
- how to ensure their own safety in the course of meetings, and travelling to and from them;
- how to ask for a legacy;
- body language (yours and theirs).

You could conduct your own training programme, or find consultants or trainers able to train in one or more of these subjects.

There are a number of books on will making available for the lay person, as well as charities' own will-making booklets. Provide your fundraisers with a referral mechanism, and encourage them to use it. Sources of further help, pages 176–78, gives more information in these two areas.

Personal security

When conducting face-to-face fundraising, the security of both fundraiser and prospect needs to be considered, but the chances of problems are remote and should not be got out of proportion.

The personal safety of the fundraiser

Employers have a duty in law to assess the risk to their employees' personal safety and to introduce appropriate measures. Employees have a duty too to comply with health and safety regulations at work. A good starting point is to consult the Suzy Lamplugh Trust (the

National Charity for Personal Safety), which has a range of useful publications on minimising risk and dealing with incidents, and can provide training (see Sources of further help, p 178). Consider seeking examples of good practice in the voluntary sector and advice from organisations such as NSPCC, which has introduced training on personal safety for its regional fundraisers and social workers.

CHECKLIST SOME BASIC SUGGESTIONS FOR PERSONAL SAFETY

- Always let your office know when and precisely where you are due to meet a prospect.
- Tell them how long you expect to be. Ring in on your journey there and on departing from the meeting.
- Consider always carrying a mobile telephone and having someone ring you in the early part of the meeting on some pretext or other, to ensure that you are all right.
- Pre-programme the telephone with emergency numbers, so that 999 and your office number can be called as easily as possible.
- Park your car facing the direction to take on leaving, to facilitate a quick getaway if required. Have only one key on your key ring – to operate the car.
- A woman due to visit a male prospect for the first time should consider being accompanied by another woman on that and future visits until she feels comfortable going alone.
- When you are in the prospect's home, make a mental note, on your arrival, of the way out and of how to operate the front door as it closes. Sit as near the door of the sitting room as possible and be alert to strange or inconsistent behaviour, or danger signals. Being aware is the key.

This checklist represents a minimum of advice. Get more!

You should dress casually but smartly, and neutrally: you don't want to intimidate the prospect by looking over-professional, nor by seeming over-prosperous, or provocative. You also need to strike the right balance between casual and professional, to establish in the prospect's mind that this is a business, not a social, call.

The security of the prospect

The prospect too needs to be, and feel, secure.

- Confirm the meeting in writing beforehand, and always show an identity card with your photograph, your name and that of the charity, even if it is not asked for.

- Think about your body language: is any aspect of it threatening?
- Relax the prospect with some initial chat.
- Do not stick rigidly to your objectives for the meeting. Go with the flow of the conversation, discreetly steering it as needed.
- Consider the dress points mentioned above.

Handling on-the-spot donations

Your charity should set a procedure for dealing with immediate donations to protect itself and you.

- Always carry a receipt book, and give the prospect an official charity receipt when handed a donation.
- Try to get a cheque (in preference to cash) and ensure it is made out to the charity, never to you personally. You can say, 'I'm sorry, I'm not allowed to accept that.'
- If handed cash, ask for it to be put in an envelope addressed by the prospect to the charity. Bank it as soon as possible (retaining the envelope) following a pre-set procedure – or take it straight to the office. Tell your prospect that is what you will do.
- On leaving the meeting, ring in to the office to report the fact of the donation and what you will do with it. Make a file note of the gift and the conversation with your office.
- Ensure that the donation is acknowledged by your charity as soon as possible. Should someone other than you do this?

The value of telephone and letter

Face-to-face meetings with prospects may be by far the most profitable (in the broadest sense of the word) method of contact, but it is important to conclude this chapter with a reminder of the value of telephone and letter contact. These forms of contact are particularly useful as a means of gathering information or priming prospects prior to meeting them face to face, or even as an alternative to doing so.

Some people may not want face-to-face contact or may regard it as an expensive and questionable use of a charity's resources. If you sense that someone is particularly interested in your administration and fundraising costs, use the telephone as an alternative. (In just such a situation, one particular charity has recently secured a substantial legacy pledge.) The telephone is also a valuable alternative if you cannot afford face-to-face work.

Some individuals can be moved to pledge purely through communication by letter. A letter is also a valuable means of communicating a lot of information (whether this concerns will making or your charity's work): you can send this either to summarise and perhaps expand on an earlier telephone conversation or to prepare the way for a future telephone call. People's lack of familiarity with the legal aspects of will making, and their tendency to put off getting down to it, make a written record of your conversation a valuable reminder.

CHAPTER THIRTEEN

Retaining pledgers' commitment and maximising giving potential

Anthony Clay

The expression 'pledger' has come to be used by charities to describe those who have remembered a charity in their will and have told the charity about this ('pledged' their bequest). With the development of legacy fundraising, more charities have discovered the benefits of keeping in touch with those who have pledged a bequest. This is the substance of this chapter, which covers the following subjects: requesting pledges, maintaining contact with pledgers, researching pledgers, encouraging supporters to make wills, and recognising and involving pledgers in support of their chosen charity *before* they die.

Asking for notification of pledges

In the 1970s, the Royal Society for the Protection of Birds (RSPB) decided to ask supporters to contact the charity when they had remembered it in their wills, so that the success of each promotion could be evaluated long before the bequest became a reality. But how could supporters be persuaded to do this? And, even if they said that they had indeed remembered the RSPB in their wills, could they be believed? At the time, Mobil had sponsored the RSPB to produce a 'coffee-table' book on the Society's bird reserves, complete with a gazetteer. It took little effort to persuade Mobil to pay for a print over-run of around one thousand copies that could then be offered as a gift to those who pledged a legacy to the RSPB and who told the Society that they had done so.

There was a concern that people might write in to say that they had remembered the RSPB in their wills when they had not, simply to get the book. The precaution was therefore taken of suggesting that they should take the response slip requesting the book to their solicitors who would then send it on to the RSPB, saying that their client had remembered the Society in their will and had asked that the book be sent on to them.

Since then, many other charities have offered inducements to pledgers. When the gift has been perceived as having a reasonably high value, substantial numbers of pledges of bequests have been received, especially where the gift has been relevant to the work of the charity concerned.

In the mid-1980s, a charity providing nursing care to former service-men and sevicewomen was receiving, more than three years into a promotion that had used incentives, over 25 per cent of its legacies from people who had pledged their bequests. That same charity now has pledges for over 60 per cent of its legacies each year, together with a further 5 per cent from people who had clearly reacted to the charity's legacy promotion without going so far as to pledge. The offer of incentives to people to pledge a bequest can therefore work well. Furthermore, the author has yet to learn of one proven case where someone who had pledged and received a gift subsequently died without leaving the charity any money.

For some charities the offer of a gift to pledgers is not practical, per-haps because there is no sensible relevant gift available or because the trustees would not countenance giving the charity's money away in such a fashion. Indeed, the majority of charities seem to be unhappy about offering an incentive, for whatever reason. However, the cost of inaction is that a charity will have to rely on those few benefactors who write to tell it of their intention – and they will remain a very small proportion of benefactors. For this reason, char-ities really should do all that they can to encourage people to pledge and to tell them about it when they have done so.

Keeping in touch with pledgers

There are good reasons why people should pledge, many of which have been given in preceding chapters. Pledging is a way of telling a charity how much an individual cares, helping the charity to make long-term plans, ensuring that the pledger's voice is heard and encouraging the charity to keep in touch. But few people will tell charities about their intentions unless they are clearly and frequently asked to do so.

Whether a charity has many pledgers or none, there are a number of reasons why it should treat its potential legators properly. It is known that some major charities are beginning to lose 'market share' to other charities, and there has been a steady rise in the number of charities sharing co-beneficiaries in charitable bequests. For exam-ple, one major national charity found itself sharing bequests with some three or four other charities ten years ago, whereas it now shares with more than five on average.

It is clearly important to keep the attention, interest and understanding of the charity and its needs in the minds of its benefactors. Here are some reasons to support this claim:

- Now that most solicitors can keep wills in electronic format, it is relatively easy to re-make a will without extensive re-typing. It is therefore cheaper and quicker than it used to be to cut a person, or a charity, out of one's will.

- The incidence of will making is increasing and intestacies declining. So the occasions when the opportunities arise to cut charities out of wills are also increasing.

- People who have left a small pecuniary sum to a charity may be persuaded to change this to a residuary bequest involving a share in their estate. Since residuary bequests are on average worth at least five times more than pecuniary bequests, this is an important objective.

- A will may contain a requirement that cannot be fulfilled, for example that a bequest be spent only on something outside the objectives of the charity. If the benefactor can be told of the problem, there may be opportunities to change the conditions.

- Adverse press comment may at any time negatively affect the public image of a charity. If that charity is in touch with its pledgers, it has a chance to counteract such adverse criticism.

- Most people will, understandably, wish to benefit mainly their families and dependants in their will. This may lead them to dismiss the idea of remembering a charity as well because they do not expect that there will be any money left over. However, it is widely known that many people die leaving far more wealth behind than they believed they had.

- Few people will remember a charity in their wills without prompting. One national charity working in the environmental field had received not a single legacy in the thirty years of its existence. Yet when it asked its 20,000 supporters whether they would consider remembering it in a future will, 16 per cent said they would.

- The value of legacies is more than five times greater, on average, than the total of lifetime gifts.

A woman died, leaving half of the residue of her estate (a little over £1 million) to the NSPCC and half to the RSPCA. She also left £30,000 to the RSPB as a pecuniary sum. Neither the NSPCC nor the RSPCA had any record of her as a donor or supporter, but she had left all of an extensive library of bird books, binoculars and so on to the RSPB. Why did she leave so little (relatively) to the RSPB and so much to the other two charities with whom she apparently had no connections?

Through contact with the executors, it was quickly established that, although the legator was a keen birdwatcher, her husband (who had died ten years earlier) was not. His interests had been in preventing cruelty to children and animals. When the lady had re-made her will following her husband's death she had thought that she would divide her estate (then worth about £100,000) three ways. She knew that the RSPB had recently bought an important bird reserve for about £30,000, so she left that amount to the birds and the remaining two-thirds equally to the other two charities which represented her late husband's interests. Shortly after that she received a large bequest from an uncle. Her estate was well managed and grew to be worth over £1 million at the time of her death.

Even charities like the National Trust and the RSPB, who operate highly efficient membership schemes, find that most of their legators were not previously known to them. What chance then will there be for charities that rely more on casual donations than membership subscriptions of knowing who their benefactors are? The answer is 'not much' – unless they work very hard at it. The remainder of this chapter, therefore, is devoted to looking at how to achieve the closest possible communications with pledgers, people who have definitely written wills containing a legacy to your charity, and people who have yet to get around to doing so.

Researching and categorising potential benefactors

Researching past legators

Probably the best way to start to understand your charity's future benefactors is to analyse its past benefactors. Fortunately, a great deal of information is contained in the files of previous estates. If you subscribe to Smee & Ford's notification services you will have a ready reference source contained in their report forms. These provide the following kind of information on legators:

- their gender;
- their location at death;

- their age at death (sometimes);
- their profession (occasionally);
- the date of their wills and the date of their death (and consequently the 'age' of their wills);
- whether they left a pecuniary or residuary bequest;
- the value of a pecuniary bequest;
- the value of their estate and, therefore, an estimate of the value of a residuary bequest;
- an indication of whether they consulted a solicitor, or bank, or accountant when making their will;
- any other charitable causes they were interested in;
- any special conditions the benefactors made or other special interests they might have had.

All this amounts to much more information about most legators than you will have about most donors. If you can match up data on bequests with what you may know about your donors from profile analysis and other research (see Chapters 6 and 7 for more information on these activities), you may be able to achieve an accurate picture of your charity's legators.

Groups of benefactors vary considerably between organisations. One national, household-name charity had an extraordinarily high number of 'home-made' wills, where solicitors had plainly not been consulted, combined with a relatively high frequency of low-value pecuniary bequests with no particular regional bias. Conversely, another had an astonishingly high average residuary bequest value, with every will appointing a solicitor or bank as executor, and a strong bias to London and the south-east. Clearly, by targeting similar people, one would expect to achieve a group of pledgers who tended to match them. Research is usually advisable to verify this.

Researching enquirers and pledgers

What motivates people to leave money to a charity? The following are some of the more likely reasons:

- strong interest in and affection for a cause;
- gratitude to the charity;
- relationship with the charity;
- a way of perpetuating memory of the benefactor;
- to continue the benefactor's influence beyond the grave;
- to make a tangible and appropriate demonstration of 'goodness';

- belief that making a charitable bequest is the 'done thing';
- to spite people who believed that they would benefit;
- to make a substantial contribution of a size which is possible only through a legacy.

How do you find out which are the most relevant reasons for your charity's benefactors? The best, and possibly the only, way is to carry out research (as is proposed, for example, in Chapter 7 of this book). Research work tends to indicate very clear differences between enquirers and pledgers, especially if enquirers have responded simply to an offer of free advice on making a will – a favourite gambit of charities in the 1980s and early 1990s.

While pledgers are more likely to be female, aged over 60, widowed or married and in the higher socio-economic groups, enquirers tend to be male, under 60, married or single, with children and in the lower socio-economic groups. Perhaps this is not surprising, because enquirers may feel that, when considering legacies at this stage of their life, their first commitment should be to family and friends.

These differences apart, both pledgers and enquirers may have a surprisingly tenuous relationship with a charity. It is often the case that even pledgers seem to have extraordinarily sketchy ideas about the charity's true nature and aspirations. They are frequently not committed supporters, so the nature of an individual's relationship with the charity may not necessarily be the most important factor in the bequest decision. A simple wish to do something to help a good cause, regardless of precisely which charity they choose, seems often to be the key. On the face of it, this may be an argument against spending too much time and money on building relationships with potential legators, but it is more likely to reflect the lack of such effort in the past than a genuine lack of interest on the part of benefactors.

Categories of enquirers and pledgers

It is clearly important to categorise enquirers into groups such as:

- casual and probably no longer interested;
- potentially interested, but not yet;
- interested, but have not yet got round to pledging;
- actual pledgers.

It is usually not easy to determine the category into which an enquirer falls. Sometimes the enquiry itself will tell a good deal about the enquirer, but mostly it will be the type of request that simply asks, 'Please send information about . . .'.

The best way to categorise enquirers is to enclose a response device with the literature you send, asking the enquirer to tell you more about themselves. This should be followed up with a further letter or, better still, a telephone call (by trained staff or volunteers) seeking a response when necessary.

Few people will object to being asked, for example, whether what they received in response to their request was relevant to their needs and generally helpful. Their answers to these questions should provide enough information for you to categorise them quite adequately and, on the strength of that, develop a sensible and appropriate legacy promotional strategy for them.

The pledgers themselves can be categorised as follows:

- low-level pecuniary benefactors, leaving legacies of, say, £100–£1,000.
- higher-level pecuniary benefactors leaving legacies of, say, £1,000 upwards;
- residuary benefactors with no apparent past interest in the charity;
- residuary benefactors with some previous, limited, involvement;
- residuary benefactors known as being very close to the charity.

The best way of categorising pledgers is to ask them to answer key questions on the pledge form itself. Some pledgers will happily tick a value box indicating which band corresponds to their pecuniary bequest; some residuary pledgers will be prepared to indicate the percentage share of their estate the charity is to receive. People will also often be prepared to give their date of birth, although they may jib at giving their age.

Pledge forms should be clearly marked 'Private and Confidential' and treated as such. Ideally, these enquirers and pledgers should be treated differently; in practice, however, the segmentation can only be approximate. However, the basic point remains that understanding of the likely different attitude of each segment is absolutely key.

Securing the legacy

Getting supporters to make wills

It is useful to understand something of the psychology associated with making a will. Unfortunately very little research has been carried out into what motivates some people, but not others, to make a will. People with no will may be suffering from a fear of confronting their own mortality; they may be ignorant of the procedure, or dislike solicitors or believe that they have not enough money to justify making a will. They may believe that there is no need to make a will because the intestacy rules will ensure that their nearest and dearest will be looked after. Often, they probably simply never get round to it.

It is extremely important to make a will, if for no other reason than that the intestacy rules are quite complex and may not be in everyone's best interest, especially if there are children. Making a will is neither difficult nor expensive, and it is usually easy to update one. Some people use the same solicitors throughout their adult lives, sometimes a trusted friend from school or university whom they appoint as executor. A problem can be that the solicitor will be way past retirement age when the will is finally administered, so it is important that people should consider appointing a younger solicitor in due course. This can be an opportunity for updating the will to include a charity – the time when most people re-make a will and include a charity for the first time is on the death of a spouse.

Some charities have found that the great majority of their supporters already have a will. This is especially the case with those over 60 years old, a group of people charities are most interested in for the purpose of promoting legacies.

The message to most charity supporters should probably focus more on the need to keep wills up to date than on the need to make a will in the first place. Modern legacy advertising has tended to move away from 'free advice on how to make a will' towards stronger emphasis on the charity and its work and how critically important legacies have been in the past and will be in future.

There is usually no obvious time of year to promote legacies. Analysis of months when wills were made shows small increases at the end of winter and the end of summer. Since this indicates the time when the wills were signed, rather than when instructions for writing the will were given, there might be an argument for stepping up legacy promotion in midwinter and midsummer.

Guarding against impossible conditions

Most bequests to charities are for general purposes, but occasionally people will specify impossible or difficult conditions. In these cases, the bequest to the charity may fail.

A useful device to avoid the imposition of impossible conditions is to ask potential legators who have specific requests to include the words 'but without imposing a binding trust', making it clear that the charity is not under a binding obligation with regard to the request in question. (There is a special legal phraseology for this.) The charity is then free not to follow the request if necessary. Conscientious solicitors tend to advise their clients against being too specific in order to guard against future problems. It would be as well for charities also to advise potential legators about the possible difficulties of being too specific and of leaving bequests that are not charitable, for example requiring the charity to use the money for political lobbying.

Securing the continued support of pledgers
Recognising the pledge

It is absolutely crucial that people who have pledged a bequest are treated differently from other donors. Although they should continue to receive the charity's literature, as a general rule they should not be sent low-level requests for donations. Increasingly, charities are making direct contact with pledgers, inviting them to receptions, giving them special treatment at meetings or events, and asking them to visit projects.

Some charities may take the view that there is no need to talk to their supporters once they have pledged, but experience shows that most pledgers welcome opportunities to learn more about the charity's work and to be treated as special. Some charities, for example, send a special mail shot to their pledgers each year, sometimes with the gift of a calendar or Christmas card (it is important to test this by researching recipients to find out whether they wish this kind of activity to continue).

Pledgers vary greatly in their desire to be contacted. The question of recognition during the pledgers' lifetime can also be tricky: most appreciate the charity's thanks but do not want their bequest to be publicised while they are still alive. To this end, many larger charities have a member of staff trained in probate work who is available to talk to pledgers about their bequests and to discuss what forms of recognition they would like.

Many forms of recognition can be offered once the pledger has died. Books, gardens and trees of remembrance are quite common, but it is important to ensure that there are adequate funds for maintaining them in the years ahead. This can be surprisingly expensive. For example, a typical crematorium in the South of England will charge £100 for one rose bush for ten years, after which it will be removed unless a new contract is taken out. It can be bad for the charity's image if items of remembrance are allowed to fall into disrepair, so it is right to point out the potential difficulties to pledgers.

Personal and professional involvement

Pledgers' expectations of what they want from the benefiting charities will, of course, vary greatly. Some will expect regular, professional contact; others may be annoyed by anything other than a simple acknowledgement. Most require at least that the charity keeps in touch and has experienced and trained staff available to answer questions and to give advice when it is sought.

Contact with pledgers can be informal or formal. Usually a successful relationship-building programme will involve invitations to a series of social events, such as receptions and project visits, combined with professional advice from a solicitor if necessary. Some charities, such as those for older people, have a natural authority to give professional advice; others will have to supplement their own ability to give advice with a fully qualified legal service.

There have been some unfortunate examples of charities who have offered a telephone advice service, which turns out to be rarely staffed or to be answered by people with little or no knowledge of the subject. Just because the questions asked of such services are usually simple and straightforward does not excuse inefficient or sloppy service. After all, with 1997 average pecuniary bequests worth £3,200 and average residuary bequests worth around £24,000, pledgers are among the most generous supporters your charity will have. Conveying your gratitude properly while they are alive, in the sure knowledge that you cannot do so after they have died, seems no more than elementary politeness.

Charities that are corporate bodies can act as executors of wills. Some may have responsibilities to look after trust funds or take responsibility for people who may, for example, have learning difficulties. In these circumstances it is necessary for the charity to have its own legal department.

Professional back-up (ie knowledge of will-making law and how to administer an estate) can be a useful way of offering help and advice to pledgers and can add authority to the charity's offers of assistance with bequests. But it is important that the charity should encourage its benefactors to seek proper professional advice. After all, most people who remember charities in their wills have estates worth more than £100,000. Simple, home-made wills are very unlikely to be adequate. This, surely, is good enough reason alone not to recommend that supporters should use the simple computerised will-writing services that are now readily available.

Charities that are not corporate bodies will not be able to act as executors. Members of staff or legal advisers may nevertheless do so as individuals on behalf of the charity, but will they still be working for the charity when the pledger dies? If they are, there are issues surrounding the time involved, expertise required and whether the charity can be remunerated. It is best not to allow employees to act as executors.

The pledger as lifetime supporter

Some pledgers will offer large gifts during their lifetime often with sentiments such as 'You might as well have it now', and occasionally pledgers will ask 'Would you like it now or later?' The danger of the charity accepting a major gift in a person's lifetime is that the donor may, when old and infirm, fall short of funds and ask to have part or all of the gift repaid – something the charity is unable to do because it is not empowered to use its funds in that way. It is always sensible to try to find out as much as possible before accepting or refusing a large lifetime gift in lieu of a legacy. The ultimate choice must, of course, be that of the individual, but people often appreciate the charity's comments and professional advice.

It is essential that pledgers should be protected from receiving 'run-of-the-mill' appeal letters from the charity. It seems highly inappropriate that someone who has pledged a bequest worth, say, well over £10,000 should receive regular requests for gifts in the usual £25–£100 range of most direct-mail appeals. By all means send them information about the charity, invite them to events and keep them as involved as they may wish to be – but to treat them just like anyone else on the mailing list shows a serious lack of understanding about just how important they are. Segmentation should be used to ensure that pledgers do not receive inappropriate offers: for example, very elderly people should not be invited to receptions miles away from where they live.

Keeping in touch with pledgers is best done through a combination of tailored letters, telephone calls and face-to-face communications from people who have studied the records and know as much as can reasonably be known of the pledgers' circumstances, interests and past giving history.

Undue influence

There is an increasing number of challenges to charitable bequests in the courts. The costs of such cases will almost always be borne by the estate, unless the challenge is fraudulent or frivolous. Bearing in mind that litigation is likely to cost a minimum of £10,000, there will always be a great pressure to settle out of court.

It has been argued that anything a charity does to communicate with potential and actual benefactors could be said to be bringing undue influence to bear (an argument that would merely serve to increase the numbers of contested bequests). Ultimately the charity's trustees must decide how far to go in promoting legacies for their cause, but charities have a duty to do everything they can to secure their future income. As long as charities confine this effort to promoting the need that they exist to serve, presenting excellent examples of the importance of past legacies, building true relationships with potential benefactors and responding to their needs for more information, there can be no good reason why they should avoid legacy promotion simply for fear of stimulating potential objections from litigious claimants.

The fact that many legators do not realise how wealthy they are when they die does not necessarily mean that they are not perfectly in control of things at the time of making their wills. Some may leave money to charity with the desire to spite individuals who might be hoping to benefit, but why should they not do this after their deaths any more than they could when they were still alive?

The future of good causes will depend upon building much closer relationships with supporters of all kinds. That means building relationships also with the older, possibly lonelier, supporters who will remember charities in their wills. If that upsets some of their more distant relatives, then so be it. Charity legators are likely to remain an especially important group of people to fundraisers. They need, and deserve, special attention.

A donor's perspective 5

Well, I have been involved with Charity X for years and years, and they do such wonderful work and have meant so much to me that, yes, I have made provision in my will to support them, because I think it's really important.

We both had a will for many years, because my husband always cared for me and said it was important that we made plans for the time when one of us wouldn't be around any longer. It was only after he died that my son sat me down and talked to me about how the original will was now invalidated and said I really ought to think about amending or making a new will, given my new circumstances.

I've been active really at all levels within Charity X over a number of years and I have talked, on and off, to some of the staff about the different types of fundraising they do and I've seen the legacy leaflets that we produce and even handed them out without ever thinking that actually they could be for me as well.

But once I had started thinking about what I would do in my own will I did have a couple of conversations with friends within Charity X and was really interested that one of them had already made a sizeable gift to the charity in his will. In fact, I even talked about it with [a fundraiser] when we were organising our annual concert, and it was she who talked to me about just how important legacies are to the work that we are doing. No, it didn't really strike me as unusual or difficult that she worked for the charity and that I was a supporter when we were talking about it. After all, I don't really see what we do in that way, anyway – we really are all in it together.

I brought home the legacy leaflet and discussed it with my son, and, while he was a bit nervous at first, he knew how much it meant to me, and to Frank, and I think he knew then that I was going to make some form of important gift.

In the end, I actually did talk with the legacy fundraiser, who was really nice and didn't pressurise me in any way and really helped me to see that it is just another way of helping the work to get done. I don't feel under any pressure and I really didn't feel that the charity was wanting me to make a legacy. I just thought it was the right thing to do.

I discussed it with our solicitor and he told me what the various options were. For me it is really important that the family and the kids are all accounted for, and they do still get the vast majority of my estate. So that's why in the end we all agreed that the best thing to do was to make a residuary gift, and that's what I've done.

I've told the charity and of course they were really pleased, and they have been really nice about it, but I have also said that I don't want any particular treatment as a result. Sometimes I might mention it when I'm in Charity X, if I'm talking with other volunteers or whatever, but to be honest, it's not the sort of thing that normally comes up in conversation. I feel pleased that I've made the gift and I think, and I know, that Frank would be pleased too, because he knows how much Charity X means to me, even more so now that I've got time on my hands and there's so much to be done.

PART 3

Legacy administration

CHAPTER FOURTEEN

The Law concerning succession to property on death

Andrew Mortimer

This chapter provides a concise guide to the law relating to all aspects of the passing of property on death, whether by will or intestacy – the situation where someone dies without a will (a death 'intestate'). Included is a detailed section on the types of gift that can be made by will (including charitable gifts), the circumstances in which they can fail (and what the consequences of failure are), and how estates are currently taxed. This chapter states the rules at the date of going to press. The applicable rules (particularly regarding tax) must be checked at the relevant time.

Wills and codicils

A will is a written statement, completed with the required formalities, setting out intentions about what is to happen on or after death. Typically a person writing a will (a testator) will deal with the appointment of executors (the people who will deal with assets and liabilities after the testator's death), the appointment of guardians for any infant children, and also who will receive any property (the estate).

A codicil is normally executed in order to add to or change the provisions of a will. There can sometimes be many codicils made to supplement a will.

The key elements of a will

There are six essential characteristics of a will or a codicil:

- It must be in writing.
- It must be made by a person over 18 years old.
- It must be made by a person having sound mind, memory and understanding, and a clear intention that it should operate after that person's death.

- It must not be made as a result of undue or improper influence.

- It must be signed by the testator; alternatively, it may be signed on the testator's behalf in the presence and at the direction of the testator. It must be clear that the testator intended to give effect to the document by signing it.

- The signature of the testator must be made or acknowledged in the presence of at least two witnesses who are present together at the same time. Two independent adults should be asked to act as witnesses. It is crucial that no beneficiary or the spouse of any beneficiary should act as a witness, since that would prevent them receiving benefits under the document. Each witness must additionally sign the document in the presence of the testator. Ideally, the document should contain a statement (an attestation clause) showing that these requirements have been complied with.

Strictly speaking, a will does not need to be dated. However, it is generally good practice to insert the date when the testator signs it.

The effect of wills and codicils

A will or a codicil only takes effect on death. Until the testator dies, the document may be revoked or altered at any time.

A person can use a will or codicil to dispose of any land and buildings (real property) and any cash, investments or other possessions (personal property) he or she owns. Wills and codicils do not, however, deal with all types of property. They cannot generally deal with property in joint names (eg a house or a bank account). The legal rule is that property in joint names passes automatically to the survivor on the death of one owner.

There may also be restrictions on the extent to which a will can deal with foreign property. The law of the country in which the property is situated may mean that it is not possible for it to be disposed of under a will. For example, a surviving spouse or children may have automatic rights to it under the law of the country where the property is situated.

There is no requirement that a will or codicil be registered, or that it be stored in any particular way. The prudent thing is to make sure that the documents are kept in a safe place, and also that the testator's family and executors know that it exists, and where it is kept.

Intestacy

Intestacy is what happens when a person dies intestate, that is leaving no effective statement of how he or she wants his or her property dealt with after death.

An intestacy can be either total or partial. Broadly speaking, total intestacy occurs when there is no effective will. Partial intestacy occurs where the will does not deal with the whole of the person's property.

Who may benefit from the estate?

On an intestacy, the family of the person who has died becomes entitled to his or her assets in the order set down in the Administration of Estates Act 1925 (as amended). The intestacy rules provide that the estate will pass as follows in the table below. The persons named in Column 1 are entitled to inherit in the order of priority stated. The 'statutory trusts' are the conditions set out in the 1925 Act, under which the beneficiaries inherit.

RIGHTS ON INTESTACY IN CASE OF DEATHS ON OR AFTER 1 DECEMBER 1993

Relatives surviving	Distribition of Estate	
	Where spouse survives	Where no surviving spouse
1 Issue	Spouse takes 1 the personal chattels, 2 £125,000 net free of inheritance tax and costs, plus interest at 6% pa until payment or appropriation, and 3 a life interest in half of the remainder of the estate, with reversion to the issue. The issue take the other half of the remainder of the estate absolutely on the statutory trusts.	All to the issue on the statutory trusts.
2 Parents	Spouse takes 1 the personal chattels, 2 £200,000 net free of inheritance tax and costs, plus interest at 6% pa until payment or appropriation, and 3 half the remainder absolutely. The parents take the remainder absolutely (in equal shares if both survive).	All to the parents (in equal shares if both survive).

3 Brothers and/or sisters of the whole blood (including the issue of any such brothers or sisters who predeceased the intestate).	Spouse takes 1 the personal chattels, 2 £200,000 net free of inheritance tax and costs, plus interest at 6% pa until payment or appropriation, and 3 half the remainder absolutely. The brothers and sisters, and issue of predeceased brothers and sisters, of the whole blood take the remainder absolutely on the statutory trusts.	All to the brothers and sisters and issue of predeceased brothers and sisters of the whole blood on the statutory trusts.
4 Brothers and/or sisters of the half blood (including the issue of any such brothers or sisters who predeceased the intestate).	All to the surviving spouse absolutely. (Whatever the size of the estate, no kin more remote than the issue of brothers or sisters of the whole blood take any interest in the estate where the deceased left a surviving spouse.)	All to the brothers of the half blood and issue of predeceased brothers and sisters of the half blood on the statutory trusts.
5 Grandparents	All to the surviving spouse absolutely.	All to the grandparents (if more than one, in equal shares).
6 Uncles and/or aunts of the whole blood (including the issue of any such uncles or aunts who predeceased).	All to the surviving spouse absolutely.	All to the uncles and aunts and issue of predeceased uncles and aunts of the whole blood on the statutory trusts.
7 Uncles and/or aunts of the half blood (including the issue of any such uncles or aunts who predeceased).	All to the surviving spouse absolutely.	All to the uncles and aunts and issue of predeceased uncles and aunts of the half blood on the statutory trusts.
8 No relative in any of the above classes who attains an absolutely vested interest.	All to the surviving spouse absolutely.	All to the Crown or to the Duchy of Lancaster or the Duke of Cornwall.

Source Butterworths (1993) *Wills Probate and Administration Services,* Vol 1, Issue 9.

The main point to note about these rules is that the surviving spouse is not automatically entitled to all the assets. The assumption that he or she is is common but mistaken.

On a partial intestacy, beneficiaries must bring into account any benefits they receive under the will in determining the application of the intestacy provisions.

Family provision: the 1975 Act

The provisions of the Inheritance (Provision for Family and Dependants) Act 1975 restricts the freedom that a person has to dispose of his or her property by way of will under English law.

Under the 1975 Act, any one of a specified class of people may apply to the Court for various orders if they can show that the provisions of the will, or the statutory intestacy rules, do not make reasonable financial provision for the person applying.

Who can apply?

The people who can apply under the 1975 Act are:

- a surviving wife or husband (even if judicially separated);
- a former wife or husband who has not re-married;
- in relation to a person dying on or after 1 January 1996, a co-habitee, that is a person who during the two years before the death lived in the same house as the deceased as the husband or wife of the deceased;
- a dependent child, including an adopted or illegitimate child;
- a person treated as a child of the family, that is a person for whom the deceased acted as a parent;
- any other person who immediately before the death was being maintained, either wholly or partly, by the deceased.

What orders can be made?

Where an application is made under the 1975 Act, the Court has to decide whether the will or the intestacy rules make reasonable financial provision for the applicant. If not, the Court then has to make an objective decision about the provision to be made.

In making this decision, the Court has to consider a number of issues specified in the 1975 Act, including: the financial resources and financial needs of the applicant both now and in the foreseeable future; the obligations and responsibilities that the deceased had towards the applicant; and the size and nature of the deceased's estate.

The Court can, among other things, order periodical payments, lump-sum payments and transfers and settlements of property. A Court order can relate to any property in the person's estate, including any property that might be left to charity under a person's will. Thus, an order under the 1975 Act can override a charitable legacy.

Executors and administrators

Personal representatives

The generic term for the person entrusted with the task of winding up a deceased person's estate is a 'personal representative' (PR). He or she is the person who steps into the shoes of the deceased and has full legal authority to deal with the estate. A PR must be over the age of 18.

Confirmation of this legal authority is given by a document called a 'grant of representation'. This is a formal document issued and sealed by the Probate Registry. Where there is a will, the document will usually be called a 'grant of probate'. Where there is an intestacy, the document will usually be called 'letters of administration'.

Normally no grant of representation is necessary where the estate is a 'small' estate, defined as below £5,000 in value.

Identifying the personal representative

It is normal practice for a will to contain an appointment of one or more persons to act as 'executor'. Typically, a person will appoint his or her spouse or children, close family friends or relations, or perhaps a solicitor or bank.

On a total intestacy, the Administration of Estates Act 1925 sets out the rules for deciding who is entitled to be the PR, or 'administrator', as they may also be called. The order of entitlement is as follows:

- surviving spouse
- children
- grandchildren
- parents
- brothers and sisters

- nephews and nieces
- grandparents
- uncles and aunts
- cousins
- the Crown
- creditors.

On a partial intestacy – where a will does not deal with the whole of a person's property – then the executors will technically act as 'administrators' in relation to the assets subject to the intestacy and will deal with them in accordance with the intestacy rules described above.

Where there is a will, but there is no valid or effective appointment of executors within it, then anyone who stands to benefit from a share of the residue of the estate, or of particular legacies of assets, can apply to act as PR. In the absence of any such person, the Crown and creditors can act.

The role of the personal representative

The job of the PR is to wind up and administer the deceased person's estate. This administration of an estate generally falls into three phases:

Information gathering

The PR should identify all the assets and liabilities in the estate, organise any necessary date-of-death valuations and identify the beneficiaries of the estate.

The application for the grant of representation

An Inland Revenue account of the estate will generally be needed if the gross value of the assets in the estate is worth more than a certain figure (£180,000 for deaths after 5 April 1996). The first step will be to complete this account and send it to the Revenue with a cheque for any inheritance tax due. The second step will be for the PR to swear or affirm a PR's oath to be submitted to the Probate Registry with the original will and codicils (if any) and a receipted Inland Revenue account (if necessary).

Winding up the estate

Once the grant of representation has been issued, the PR will have legal authority to act as such. The PR will be able to close bank accounts and sell assets, including the deceased's house or any land.

The PR will pay all outstanding liabilities and expenses, settle any legacies and pay what is left of the estate to the residuary beneficiaries. The PR may often prepare final estate accounts for the beneficiaries to show what has happened.

The duties of the personal representative

The overriding duty of the PR is to wind up and administer the estate according to law and in accordance with the will or the intestacy provisions. Although technically not a trustee, the PR shares many of the duties of trustees. He or she will be obliged to act as a 'prudent man of business', and to take appropriate advice on what should be done. He or she must act in the best interests of the estate and the beneficiaries, and be prepared to account for all actions and for what he or she has done with all the assets in the estate. (Chapter 16 describes executorship service in more detail.)

Legacies and gifts

Generally speaking, people are free to dispose of property and assets under their will to whomsoever they would like to benefit from it. However, under the Inheritance (Provision for Family and Dependants) 1975 Act a testator's spouse or children or dependants may be entitled to make claims if they are not adequately provided for under the will.

Gifts of assets under the wills and codicils fall into two main types:

- First, there are legacies of particular assets (such as land, buildings or personal possessions) or cash sums. Gifts of land and buildings are also called 'devises'. Gifts of particular personal possessions are often called 'specific legacies', and gifts of cash are called 'pecuniary legacies'.

- Secondly, there are gifts of all or part of the residue of a person's estate (a 'residuary legacy' or 'devise'). The beneficiary (called a 'residuary legatee' or 'devisee') may be given a particular share or percentage of the residue.

It will be up to the PRs to decide how residuary legacies will be paid. They may sell all the assets in the estate and pay out the net cash proceeds. Alternatively, they may transfer particular assets in the residuary estate (eg stock and shares) to satisfy a residuary legacy. This is called 'appropriation'.

Conditional and reversionary gifts

Gifts in a will may be made 'conditional': that is, they will take effect only if a particular condition is satisfied. For example, a child may have to reach the age of 18 or 25 before being able to inherit.

Gifts may also be 'reversionary'. In other words, the gift will take effect subject to a prior interest. For example, under his will a husband may leave his assets to be held on trust after his death to pay income to his wife for the rest of her life, with the assets ultimately to be inherited by his children or a charity. The gift to the children or charity is reversionary and will take effect only after the wife's death.

It is crucial that the conditions attaching to a gift, or the terms setting out when it will take effect, are carefully and effectively drafted.

Charitable legacies

A legacy to a charity must be clearly drafted. The particular charitable body or purpose should be clearly identified, and the PR should check that the body or purpose is truly 'charitable' under English law. Registration with the Charity Commission is, of course, conclusive evidence that a body or purpose is charitable.

If the intention is that the charity should use the gift for a particular purpose or appeal, then this should be carefully and clearly expressed. If the gift is intended for the general benefit of the charity, it should be stated that the gift is for the 'general charitable purposes' of the charity.

Failure of legacies and gifts

General rules

Gifts may fail in a number of circumstances, including the following:

- The beneficiary died before the testator.
- The gift was subject to a condition (eg that the beneficiary reaches a particular age) which is not satisfied.
- The asset subject to the gift was no longer owned by the testator at his or her death.
- The beneficiary or his or her spouse acted as a witness to the will.
- The beneficiary may disclaim the gift.
- The will or codicil may have been wrongly witnessed or may fail to meet the required formalities.

If a gift of a particular asset fails, the result may be that the asset will form part of the deceased's residuary estate. If the gift that has failed is a gift of residue, the intestacy rules will apply if the will does not provide for what happens if a gift of residue fails. Wills should, however, ideally be drafted to cover all eventualities.

Failure of charitable legacies and the 'cy pres' rule

A gift to a charity may fail in a number of circumstances, for example:

- The charity identified in the will has ceased to exist or may never have existed.
- The objects of the charity cannot be carried out.
- The charity cannot be identified from the will.
- The gift is expressed for a particular charitable purpose, which can no longer be carried out.

However, even if there is potential failure, an application may be made to a Court to save the gift if certain conditions are satisfied. This is called the 'cy pres' rule – a term derived from the French term 'si près' (so near) and denoting the interpretation of a will as near as possible to the testator's intentions.

The Court will first of all need to be satisfied that the testator had general charitable intention, in other words a clear purpose to benefit charity. If this over-riding intention can be identified, the Court will seek to give effect to it, even if the particular way of giving effect to it stated in the will has proved impossible.

Secondly, the Court will need to be satisfied that it can find another way of carrying out the testator's general charitable intention as close as possible to the way specified by the testator. For example, if the will contains a gift for the general charitable purposes of a charity that has ceased to exist, the executors may be able to ask the Court to order the gifts to be applied 'cy pres', in other words to another charity whose objects closely resemble those of the charity that has ceased to exist.

On the other hand, if a legacy is expressly for a purpose that the charity has already carried out, or for a special appeal that has ended, then it may be difficult for a Court to find *general* charitable intention, and the gift will fail.

It is entirely up to the Court to consider whether a 'cy pres' application may be made. The Court will look at all the circumstances – including the actual terms of the will – to see whether the testator had general charitable intention. A legacy expressed for the 'general charitable purpose' of a charity may assist a Court in finding general charitable intention.

In view of the 'cy pres' rule it is critical to ensure that legacies to charities are correctly drafted, and it is generally preferable to avoid legacies limited to specific purposes or appeals that it may not be possible to carry out at the date of death.

Taxation of estates – an overview

Pre-death tax

The PRs will be responsible for ensuring that the pre-death tax affairs of the deceased are sorted out. They should ensure that tax returns up to the date of death are filed with the Inland Revenue, where required, that all income and capital gains tax is paid, and that all necessary claims for repayment are made.

Income tax post-death

The PRs will be responsible for paying income tax during the period of administration of the estate. They will generally have to account for any income arising to the residuary beneficiaries who will generally be taxable on the income in their own right.

Capital gains tax post death

For capital gains tax purposes, all assets in a person's estate will be re-valued as at the date of his or her death. All pre-death gains will be wiped out, and the beneficiaries inheriting the assets will use the value of those assets at the date of death as the value for calculating any future gains.

Any capital gains arising in the estate during the course of administration – for example on the sale of shares – will be payable by the PRs.

Inheritance tax

For inheritance tax purposes, a person is treated as making a taxable transfer of all his or her assets at the date of death. The value of certain gifts made by the deceased during the seven years before death – for example, gifts to other individuals – will also be taken into account on his or her death and made subject to inheritance tax.

The current rules provide for two rates of tax. The rate of tax applying to the value of a person's assets up to £223,000 (from 6 April 1998) is zero per cent. The rate applying to assets over that figure is 40 per cent.

There are various exemptions that may put assets outside the scope of inheritance tax altogether. Gifts between spouses are exempt, so if a husband leaves all his assets to his wife on his death, all those assets will be exempt from inheritance tax. Similarly any gifts to charity are exempt from inheritance tax.

Charities

Where a charity benefits from a person's estate, the charity should be entitled to reclaim from the Inland Revenue any income tax on income arising during the course of the administration of the estate belonging to the charity.

For inheritance tax purposes, as explained above, all gifts to charities are exempt. A difficulty can arise, however, where part of a person's estate passes to charity and is exempt from inheritance tax, but part is not. The general rule under the Inheritance Tax Act 1984 is that any inheritance tax must be borne by the non-exempt gift.

For example, say a person leaves £500,000 to be divided between a charity and her daughter. Assuming that the 0 per cent inheritance tax band has been used up by lifetime gifts, the £500,000 is subject to a 40 per cent rate of inheritance tax, but the total inheritance tax bill turns out to be £100,000. This is because the gift to the charity is exempt, so the total inheritance tax payable is 40 per cent of the half (£250,000) passing to the daughter. The application of the rules in the 1984 Act described above requires the £100,000 to be deducted from the daughter's share. Thus the daughter will receive £150,000, and the charity £250,000.

A testator may be astonished at the result of this rule. The intention may well have been, in the example above, that the £100,000 should be taken out of the estate, leaving the remainder (£400,000) to be divided equally between the daughter and the charity. The testator may be equally astonished to find that the 1984 Act expressly prevents the terms of a will overriding this rule.

This question has been subject recently to a case (*Benham's Will Trust*), where the charity involved was the RNLI. The Court in that case decided that, if a testator intended to achieve equality between his residuary beneficiaries – for example, if the testator described above intended that her daughter and the charity should benefit equally – then the Court will, if the will is properly drafted, effectively ignore the rules of the 1984 Act and give effect to those intentions.

How this would be done in the example described above is to gross up the gift to the daughter to allow for the tax that the 1984 Act says it must bear. On the figures mentioned above, the daughter would notionally be allocated £312,500 of the residue. After deducting 40 per cent on that figure, that leaves £187,500 which would be equal to the amount received by the charity.

This case is obviously of major concern to charities. Concern has been expressed by some legal commentators as to the validity of the decision on *Benham*. Pending further legislation or an appeal, it is essential that wills containing gifts to charities and other non-exempt beneficiaries should be drafted with extreme care and that testators should be advised on how exactly they would like the residue divided up.

If *Benham* is correct, then there is a very real possibility of claims by non-exempt beneficiaries against PRs who have, simply by reference to the 1984 Act, mistakenly allocated inheritance tax and divided up the estate between them and charities or other exempt beneficiaries.

CHAPTER FIFTEEN

Legacy administration systems

Hector Mullens

This chapter gives an overview of how the administration of an estate is conducted and demonstrates the importance of capturing as much information as possible about those who give a legacy to a charity, so that this can be analysed and used to inform any future legacy fundraising campaign.

Office administration

If you have the budget for one, it is worth considering an investment in a computerised legacy administration system. The specification and implementation processes themselves are useful for focusing attention on what you are doing, and how you do it, and use of such a system can streamline office procedures and improve file management capabilities. Computerising means that progress on a file can be more easily managed, and legacy data relevant to the fundraising processes or financial planning more easily obtained.

It is usually possible to find legacy administrators at charities who are willing to discuss the merits of the systems they use, and to demonstrate them to you. The information you gain from this process will be invaluable.

Even if you decide that you cannot justify or afford investment in a computerised system at the moment, then you should have a manual administration system that contains the following:

- Master index – containing name of the deceased, their address with postcode, date of death, date of will, age, type of bequest.
- Review index – this could be created in either card or book form and should prevent any individual file being overlooked where action on the part of the charity is necessary.
- Legacy cash book – to record the daily income which can then be agreed for the charity's weekly or monthly income.

- Files – although some charities will deal with only a handful of cases each year, it may be worth considering colour co-ordinating the files containing the various categories of bequest, just in case the number of bequests increases (as you would hope they would).

- Large bequests – here again it may be worth considering monitoring these separately through the use of either a book review or card index system.

- Solicitors' index – although it is possible either to purchase such an index through one of the major list brokers or to compile one by dissecting a publication such as Butterworth's *Law Directory*, it is also possible for a charity to build this up by itself simply by indexing the names of firms with which it is in correspondence on a particular case. Once established, this index can be used to note individual estates against the appropriate firm, as well as acting as a reminder when you are confronted with a firm you know tends to sit on probate cases. If your charity were to decide, as a PR exercise, to do a mailshot to solicitors, they then would have the basic list already available.

Timetable of events

On the death of a legator to your charity, you might hope to hear from the executor/bank/solicitors fairly quickly, but this by no means always happens. One sure way of finding out if your charity is mentioned in an individual's will is to subscribe to the service provided by Smee & Ford, who are a probate research agency. The company inspects every will on which a Grant of Probate is issued and will subsequently advise any charity mentioned therein. If the charity has not already been advised of its entitlement, this then enables the charity to direct a letter of enquiry to whomever is dealing with the administration.

Executors and administrators have a year from the date of death before beneficiaries can require them to distribute assets to those entitled to them. This is called the 'executor's year'. From the end of the year, a beneficiary entitled to a pecuniary legacy (which is not subject to any condition) is also entitled to interest on the unpaid legacy from the first anniversary of the death to the date of payment. If there is going to be some delay in payment of a legacy, the executor should advise the beneficiary of this.

In the case of a residuary entitlement, you can generally assume that the average estate will take one or two years to complete, but naturally there will be exceptions (for instance, the individual may have been a member of Lloyds, in which case further delay would be likely). As a residuary beneficiary, your charity is entitled to (and should ask for) a full copy of the will and any codicil thereto, and also a schedule of the assets and liabilities.

If a charity is advised that it is to receive a reversionary entitlement, this will mean, generally speaking, that a person or persons are life tenants. If possible, you should endeavour to ascertain the tenants' age, as this will then assist you in forward financial planning, even though you may conclude that you will not receive your entitlement for twenty or more years ahead. It is essential that you ascertain the nature of the assets that form a trust fund: the last thing you would wish to see is the capital assets placed in a bank or building society account. There is an obligation bestowed upon trustees to strike a balance between a reasonable return of income for the life tenants and also an element of capital appreciation for the remaindermen (those entitled to the property when the life tenant dies). However, do check the will thoroughly, since the trustees may have complete discretionary powers bestowed upon them as to the nature of the assets. A general rule of thumb (subject to the age of the life tenant) would be to make a general enquiry every five years to ascertain that the life tenant continues to enjoy the income of the trust and to be advised of any changes in the assets of the trust fund or indeed the trustees themselves. A word of caution: where there is a sole trustee who is also the life tenant, the charity should make strong representations that an additional independent trustee be appointed.

How to carry out an administration

Some charities have the status of a trust corporation, which means that the corporate body can be appointed executor and trustee of a will and undertake all that this role involves in administering an estate. The charity would generally be expected to register the death and make the funeral arrangements, to advise family and friends of such details and to send a representative of the charity to attend the burial or cremation service.

The main task then begins of verifying the assets and liabilities leading to a Grant of Probate being obtained. At the time of writing, trust corporations do not have the right to seek such a grant directly and would need to obtain this via their solicitors. Subject to what is involved, they could then either leave the continuing administration with their solicitors or undertake this themselves, thereby greatly reducing testamentary expenses. It follows that to accept such an appointment would be advantageous only if the charity is one of the main beneficiaries. While a charity is entitled to seek reimbursement of disbursements (eg telephone and postage costs), it cannot charge a fee for acting in this capacity, as this would then adversely affect the tax reliefs it would receive as a registered charity. If the charity undertakes the administration itself, it should not mix estate monies with the charity's general monies, particularly when the charity is not the sole residuary beneficiary. Detailed accounts will need to be produced and any tax matters completed to the satisfaction of the deceased's Inland Revenue district office.

If the charity has a beneficial interest in real property that forms an asset of the estate, it will generally be advised that this is to be placed for sale on the open market; in these circumstances, the charity should request particulars of the sale produced by the agents engaged to find a purchaser. Given the state of the property market generally, the charity could suggest to the solicitors acting on behalf of the executor that they would prefer to see two firms of agents handling the sale, with the commission naturally being payable on a split basis.

On being notified of the legator's death, it is the duty of the executors to ensure that the house is secure. This can be done either by the executor in person, by instructing a solicitor or an estate agent to do the job, or perhaps by relying on a friend or family member to do so. Another duty associated with making the house secure is to remove any valuables. Water storage tanks should be drained, or the services of a plumber engaged to do so. It is incumbent on the charity to see that the best price possible is obtained on a sale. The charity should therefore ask the agents engaged to give a formal confirmation that they will recommend the acceptance of such an offer, subject to contract.

Even though there will generally be a trust for sale embodied in a will, if a charity happens to be the sole residuary beneficiary, and furniture and effects are included therein, then the charity could ask the acting solicitors if they would agree to the charity taking over such items *in specie* (ie the items themselves, as distinct from their sale proceeds) either for use within the objects of the charity or to arrange their sale through their gift shop outlets.

Where a charity is executor, having obtained a valuation of the contents, it can auction those items that it is advised are worth selling by that means, and use a house clearance company for the remainder.

Tax relief

It is essential that the charity ensures that all tax reliefs to which they are entitled are correctly applied. This would cover inheritance tax, capital gains tax and income tax. It should never be assumed that these reliefs will automatically be given (for even solicitors make mistakes). It is not unknown for larger charities to produce a leaflet or memorandum to send to the firm of solicitors or equivalent when first communicating about a bequest.

Inheritance tax

It is not unknown for problems to arise with inheritance tax where, on the eventual distribution, no allowance has been made for the charitable relief. The situation can arise where beneficiaries include both private individuals and charities, 'non-exempt' and 'exempt beneficiaries'.

Capital gains tax

It may be possible to transfer to a beneficiary assets in the estate in satisfaction of their legacy. Alternatively, in the case of a charity, if an asset (such as stocks and shares) has to be sold to pay a legacy, and capital gains tax is payable as a result, then it would be sensible for the executors to transfer the asset to the charity. The charity can then sell it and take advantage of the fact that, as a charity, it is exempt from capital gains tax.

Income tax

Charities are exempt from income tax. When executors pay the income arising during an administration period to the beneficiaries they do so net of income tax. They should give the beneficiaries concerned a certificate of deduction of tax in form R185E. A charity beneficiary can then use this to reclaim the tax paid on its income. You should ask the executors for the certificate if it is not automatically provided.

Other matters arising

Lay executors

In some cases non-professional executors may indicate that they propose to deal with the administration themselves (and of course they have an absolute right to do so). In these cases, the charity should offer the executor whatever assistance it is able to, particularly in those areas where tax liabilities may arise. Other situations may develop where it would be necessary to seek legal advice. In such circumstances, instead of instructing a firm of solicitors that may not be known to either party, why not consider involving the charity's solicitors? That way costs could be kept to a minimum. Even if the lay executor did not require any assistance, it would nonetheless be a good public relations exercise to keep in touch on a regular basis.

Disputed legacies

From time to time a charity will become involved in an estate where a legal claim is lodged, usually by the surviving spouse or a child of the marriage but occasionally by other parties, under the Inheritance (Provision for Family and Dependants) Act 1975. Co-habitees of deceased people may now also claim, where the claimant and the deceased lived together for a period in excess of two years. The charity has the right to negotiate and compromise such a claim without reference to the Charity Commissioners, subject to their being satisfied that they have received all the independent advice required to achieve this. The starting point for consideration of a claim by a charity is the 1975 Act mentioned above. Where there is more than one charity involved, it is obviously sensible for one charity to instruct its own solicitors to act on behalf of all the charities involved.

Ex-gratia payments

It is not unusual for charities to be asked to make *ex-gratia* payments, but extreme caution should be taken in this area since charities generally have no authority to do so under their constitution. Following the enactment of the Charities Act 1993 a charity that feels there is justification in making such a payment must have this approved by the trustees, who must then submit an application to the Charity Commission seeking their approval for such a payment to be made (see the booklet produced by the Charity Commissioners for England and Wales, CC7 *Ex Gratia Payments by Charities*).

Information for research and strategy planning

This book has already explained how valuable the information contained in a legacy administrator's files can be to the legacy fundraising effort (see, for example, Chapters 6 and 7). All that needs to be emphasised here is how beneficial it is for the research phase of a legacy fundraising strategy to have a clear picture of the type of people your legators are, and of having the systems in place to collect this information.

Specialist skills of legacy administration

The jobs of legacy administration and legacy fundraising should not be given to the same person, as they are in some charities. While it is very important that the two functions should be closely linked, they require different skills and suit different temperaments. Legacy fundraising should be undertaken by a fundraiser, legacy administration by someone in the finance department, as either all or part of their job.

The nature of administering an estate, and the fact that even professionals like solicitors make mistakes (which can cause charities to lose out), make it important that a legacy administrator has good knowledge of wills, probate and administration law and practice. You can recruit this expertise, or you can grow it internally through research and reading, attendance on courses and seminars, and through networking with members of the inter-charity Legacy Officers Group.

Further information

There are various sources of information available that will assist even the most experienced legacy administrator: a selection of these are listed at the end of this volume (see pp 176–77).

CHAPTER SIXTEEN

Executorship services

Sebastian Wilberforce

The final chapter of this book describes the options available when choosing an executor – someone to give effect to the contents of a will.

Introduction

Care is needed when choosing executors: they may well have control of substantial funds and – although they ultimately have to account for their actions in distributing the estate – they will for a time have almost absolute discretion in what happens to those funds. The office of executor is also a burden, and the responsibilities can be extremely onerous.

The welfare of the testator's (or will-maker's) chosen beneficiaries might depend entirely upon the good sense or otherwise of an executor's actions, so a testator should be diligent in the choice of executor. That choice is between one or more of the following:

- a private individual – usually a family member or friend;
- a professional person – such as a solicitor or accountant;
- a trust corporation – such as a clearing bank, some charities, or the Public Trustee.

An important point, mentioned in previous chapters but worth reiterating here, is that wills should be professionally written. Homemade wills are a fruitful source of family dispute and even, in some cases, litigation. Having a will professionally drawn up does not *guarantee* a problem-free administration, but it does minimise the risk of something going wrong. It is a false economy to save a solicitor's fee for writing a will by writing it oneself. It is very easy to use ambiguous or unclear language or to miss out important provisions; the cost of rectifying mistakes could be many times the cost of using a solicitor in the first place.

Individuals as executors

If the intention is to appoint a private individual, given the amount of work that may be involved, it is advisable to discuss the appointment of the person concerned before naming them as executor. The individual needs to be business-like, trustworthy, and someone whose appointment will not cause conflict with other family members or the beneficiaries.

It is generally sensible to appoint two individuals as executors, in case one or other of them is unable or unwilling to act (through ill health, for example). In addition, at least one individual should be younger than the testator, in case the other appointee dies first (but remember that a child cannot act as an executor until the age of 18 years).

Private individuals can appoint a professional (whether solicitor or trustee bank) to act on their behalf.

If an individual wants to do the work personally, there are useful publications available, some of which are listed at the end of this book. The Principal or District Probate Registries will generally help with the completion of the necessary forms, and the Inland Revenue and Capital Taxes Office will give advice. Most legacy administrators at the major charities will give advice too. A private individual should be under no illusion, however, as to the amount of work involved and the possible complexity of even what may seem a straightforward estate.

Professional executors

If you want to appoint a professional executor, you should discuss doing so with whomsoever you have in mind. Consider cost, experience (different from expertise) and empathy with the beneficiaries of the will. Location is also important: you will need to take account of where a surviving spouse lives, for example, and try to ensure that the administration can be handled locally (banks tend to have central administrations). It is worth contacting several solicitors if you don't already have one; you can ask a particular solicitor to be executor if, for instance, you like their sympathetic but business-like approach or think they will handle beneficiaries well.

Appointing a professional executor to act *in conjunction with* a relative or friend has several advantages. While the professional deals with legal technicalities, the lay executor can perform the more sensitive tasks (arranging the funeral, clearing the house, and so on), for which a solicitor or bank would charge. By appointing a private executor, as well as a professional, it is also easier to keep control of both the costs and the speed at which the estate is administered.

Charities as executors

A charity can act as executor only if it has trust corporation status. Although there is nothing to prevent a particular charity employee being named as executor, this should not be encouraged. The employee may not have sufficient technical expertise or, indeed, may no longer be employed by the charity when the appointment takes effect.

As an executor, the charity can either administer estates in house or, if necessary, appoint a local solicitor to act on its behalf. Either way, the charity has a greater measure of control over costs than would normally be the case.

There is something to be said for charities providing an executorship service. A charity's ability to do so can be a key incentive for its receipt of a legacy. It also gives the charity the 'whip hand' as far as speed and efficiency of administration are concerned, whether in house or using an external agency.

Anyone considering appointing a charity should be encouraged to discuss doing so with the charity beforehand. The appointment should be accepted only where a significant legacy to the charity is contemplated. If the costs of administering the estate exceed the benefit received, the charity may lay itself open to censure for misuse of charitable funds. On the testator's death, a charity (like any other executor) can always decline its appointment, provided it has not 'intermeddled' in (ie begun to deal with) the estate.

A charge can be made against the estate to cover the cost of the administration. However, legal advice should be sought on this point before offering a full executorship service. The aim should be purely to cover costs. It is inadvisable for a charity to run the operation on a profit-making basis, since that would be a non-charitable activity.

The Public Trustee

The Public Trustee was created by Act of Parliament in 1906 to provide an executor and trustee service on a non-profit-making basis to the general public. Appointment of the Public Trustee as executor is particularly worth considering when there is no other person available to act or where the natural choice, such as a surviving spouse, is too infirm for the role. Further information on the role, responsibilities and charges of the Public Trustee can be obtained from the address given at the end of this book.

Sources of further help

Publications

There are no current publications devoted to legacy fundraising alone. Some books such as Sam Clarke's *The Complete Fundraising Handbook* (Directory for Social Change, in association with ICFM) contain chapters on the subject, but they will be of only moderate value to the reader of this detailed work.

Ken Burnett's *Friends for Life* (White Lion Press, 1997, 0171 490 4939) contains a detailed and useful chapter on legacy fundraising. He uses RNIB's legacy fundraising as a case study.

The ICFM publishes codes of practice from time to time. A full list is given on page 185.

The lead title in this CAF/ICFM Fundraising Series may well be of assistance:

Mullin R (1997) *Fundraising Strategy*. West Malling: CAF.

On will making, administering an estate and what to do when someone dies, the Consumers' Association publishes two titles that are worth investigating:

Elmhirst P, Nicholls Dr D and Rankin A J (1997) *Which? Consumer Guide to Wills and Probate*. 2nd edn. ISBN 0–85202–643–9. London: Consumers' Association.

Harris P (1997) *What To Do When Someone Dies*. Revised edn. ISBN 0–85202–647–1. London: Consumers' Association.

There is also a useful and detailed booklet produced by the Department of Social Security called *What To Do Following A Death*.

Finding and using a solicitor

Most firms do wills and probate work. The best means of finding a firm is through word of mouth. Alternatively there are various directories (the Law Society's Directory, for instance). Don't forget the database of solicitors your legacy administrator has compiled.

The Office for the Supervision of Solicitors (8 Dormer Place, Leamington Spa, CV32 5AE, tel: 01926 820082) produces leaflets on how to make a complaint against a solicitor, and how to challenge their fees.

Solicitors who practise charity law can be found through the Charity Law Association (Secretary: Anne-Marie Piper), ℅ Paisner & Co, Bouverie House, 154 Fleet Street, London EC4A 2DQ.

Legacy administration

1   The Charity Legacy Officers' Group

This is an informal gathering of professional legacy administrators. With the emphasis on legacy administration, the Group provides a useful forum for discussion of common areas of interest for all Legacy Officers. For those new to the field, it also acts as a very effective means of increasing both technical knowledge and network contacts. The current joint Chair of the Group are:

Mrs Linda Norgrove
Legacy Manager
RSPCA
Causeway
Horsham
West Sussex
RH12 1HG
tel: 01403 264181

Mrs Mary Mitchison
Legacy Manager
MacMillan Cancer Relief
15–19 Britten Street
London
SW3 3TZ
tel: 0171 351 7811

2   Conferences

Conferences on various topics are arranged regularly by Smee & Ford, by the Institute of Legal Executives and by some solicitors' firms. These seminars are widely advertised and, in general, are strongly recommended as a means of increasing specialist and technical skills.

Legacy marketing

Legacy fundraisers have their own informal forum – the Legacy Marketing Group – which meets once every two months. Further details are available from Crispin Ellison, British Heart Foundation, 14 Fitzhardinge Street, London W1H 4DH (tel: 0171 935 0185). At the time of publication, membership stands at over 90 charities.

Training sources

Ask ICFM, the Directory for Social Change and Smee & Ford for details of current courses. Some course providers will tailor courses to the needs of individual organisations.

Useful addressess

CAF (Charities Aid Foundation)
Kings Hill
West Malling
Kent
ME19 4TA
tel: 01732 520000

Capital Taxes Office
Ferrers House
PO Box 38
Castle Meadow Road
Nottingham
NG2 1BB
tel: 0115 974 6206

Charity Commission
St Alban's House
57–60 Haymarket
London
SW1Y 4QK
tel: 0171 210 4556

Inland Revenue
Charity Division
St John's House
Merton Road
Bootle
Merseyside
L69 9BB
tel: 0151 472 6000

Inland Revenue
Information Centre
Ground Floor
South West Wing
Bush House
Strand
London
WC2B 4RD
tel: 0171 438 6420

ICFM (Institute of Charity Fundraising Managers)
Fifth Floor
Market Towers
1 Nine Elms Lane
London
SW8 5NQ
tel: 0171 627 3436

Public Trust Office
24 Kingsway
London
WC2B 6JX
tel: 0171 269 7000

Smee & Ford Ltd
St George's House
195–200 Waterloo Road
London
SE1 8UX
tel: 0171 928 4050

Suzy Lamplugh Trust
14 East Sheen Avenue
London
SW14 8AS
tel: 0181 392 1839

Glossary of terms used

The following terms are used in the book.

Legal terms

Asset Any property or belonging owned by the testator.

Beneficiary A person or organisation who will benefit from your will.

Chattels Belongings such as furniture, car, etc.

Codicil A document containing a change or addition made to an existing will.

Conditional legacy A gift subject to the fulfilment of a condition (eg 'I leave my car to my eldest son on the condition he passes his A levels').

Crown The State. If you have no will and no relatives, your estate goes to the Crown.

Debts or liabilities Monies owed or outstanding (eg tax, last gas and electricity bills, hire purchase arrangements).

Discretionary trust A discretionary trust arises where property is left in a will to trustees who have the discretion to decide who should receive it. Their discretion may be limited in some way expressly by the will, or the testator may have issued private guidance to them by means of a separate 'letter of wishes'.

Estate Everything you own at the time of death.

Executors The people or organisations you have appointed to handle your affairs according to your will. The female form of the word is executrix.

Gift Aid A form of tax relief on lump sum gifts, currently of not less than £250.

Intestate If someone dies without making a will they are said to have died intestate. If they make a will that fails to dispose of all their property, a partial intestacy arises, because their will is incomplete.

Legacy/bequest A term used to describe a gift in a will. A sum of money is known as a pecuniary legacy. A specific item is known as a specific bequest.

Lifetime gift A gift made during your lifetime.

Pecuniary legacy A sum of money left in a will.

Probate The legal procedure to establish that a will is valid and genuine, and by which the executors are given the authority to act.

Residuary legacy A gift of the residue of an estate, usually expressed as a percentage or fraction.

Residue What's left of your estate after all debts and expenses have been deducted, and all bequests have been paid (except residuary legacies).

Reversionary interest A gift of property subject to a prior interest. For example, say a house has been given to someone for the rest of their life: on their death, the house goes to a charity (the charity has been given a 'reversionary interest' in the house).

Testator The person making the will. The female form of the word is testatrix.

Non-legal terms

Prospect Someone who is (or is intended to be) a recipient of the attention of legacy fundraisers up to the point at which he or she decides to leave a legacy in his or her will to the charity in question (or decides not to). The use of the term 'cold', 'warm' or 'hot' prospect denotes the perceived warmth of the prospect to the organisation or to its cause.

Pledger A person who tells a charity that he or she is intending to write a legacy to it into his or her will, or has already done so. Some organisations include within the definition of pledger someone who is considering doing so. A further distinction is frequently made between pledgers (those who have made a will including a legacy to a particular charity and have told that charity that they have done so) and 'intending pledgers' or 'possible pledgers'. Pledgers of whatever category justify more personalised attention from the fundraising charity.

Legator Someone who has died and left a legacy to charity in his or her will.

'Pennies from heaven' The expression used to denote legacies to a charity that it has not anticipated.

The editor is grateful to the cancer charity, Cancer BACUP, for allowing him to reproduce here his work from its will-making guide.

About CAF

CAF, Charities Aid Foundation, is a registered charity with a unique mission – to increase the substance of charity in the UK and overseas. It provides services that are both charitable and financial which help donors make the most of their giving and charities make the most of their resources.

Many of CAF's publications reflect the organisation's purpose: *Dimensions of the Voluntary Sector* offers the definitive financial overview of the sector, while the *Directory of Grant Making Trusts* provides the most comprehensive source of funding information available.

As an integral part of its activities, CAF works to raise standards of management in voluntary organisations. This includes the making of grants by its own Grants Council, sponsorship of the Charity Annual Report and Accounts Award, seminars, training courses and the Charities' Annual Conference, the largest regular gathering of key people from within the voluntary sector. In addition, Charitynet is now established as the leading Internet site on voluntary action.

For decades, CAF has led the way in developing tax-effective services to donors, and these are now used by more than 150,000 individuals and 2,000 of the UK's leading companies. Many are also using CAF's CharityCard, the world's first debit card designed exclusively for charitable giving. CAF's unique range of investment and administration services for charities includes the CafCash High Interest Cheque Account, two common investment funds for longer-term investment and a full appeals and subscription management service.

CAF's activities are not limited to the UK, however. Increasingly, CAF is looking to apply the same principles and develop similar services internationally, in its drive to increase the substance of charity across the world.

Other publications from CAF

Dimensions of the Voluntary Sector 1997

Key facts, figures, analysis and trends
Editor Cathy Pharoah
ISBN 1–85934–035–0 £30
Published June 1997

An easy-to-use storehouse of facts, figures and critical thinking, *Dimensions of the Voluntary Sector* provides up-to-date information on the 'third sector' which brings in over £12 billion and employs 400,000 people.

The definitive publication on the income and resources of the sector in the UK, it is widely regarded as an essential tool for busy managers, practitioners and academic researchers alike.

Completely redesigned in order to present statistics in an easily accessible and attractive form, it includes data on, among other topics:

- the top fundraising charities;
- the top corporate donors;
- the top grant-making trusts;
- the patterns in National Lottery funding.

Other, more specialised, tables analyse the performance of the NHS trusts, local authority support for charities and funding to black groups.

The Non-Profit Sector in the UK *1st edition*

ISBN 1–85934–037–7 £9.95
Published July 1997

This retrospective overview has been written for everyone interested in the role, activities and public profile of the non-profit sector in the UK in 1996. It provides a commentary on the major issues and events which have shaped the past 12 months for British non-profit organisations and assesses the impact on their work.

Supported by extensive background material on the legal and fiscal framework in which non-profit organisations operate, the distinguished authors examine the key developments in the political, social and economic areas.

Among many others, topics addressed include the transfer of the VSU to the Department of National Heritage (now the Department for Culture, Media and Sport) and the publication of the Deakin Report on the future of the sector and the changing role of volunteering.

Comprehensive coverage of fundraising issues, including the continuing debate surrounding the impact of the National Lottery and the growing importance of trading, is also provided.

The CAF/ICFM Fundraising Series
Fundraising Strategy

Redmond Mullin
ISBN 1–85934–056–3 £14.95

This is the lead title within the series, which aims to contribute to the intellectual development of fundraising theory and support the mobilisation of resources for the non-profit sector in the UK and overseas.

Fundraising today demands a substantial commitment of people, resources and marketing. Rigorous, strategic planning is a prerequisite if a campaign is to achieve success and a viable return on investment.

This book aims to clarify the principle and process of strategy and to demonstrate its place in fundraising campaigns.

To order any of the above publications please ring Biblios Publishers' Distribution Services Ltd on 01403 710851.

About ICFM

The Institute of Charity Fundraising Managers (ICFM) is the only organisation which exists to represent and support the professional interests of fundraisers at all levels. ICFM welcomes membership applications from all those working in a fundraising role or consultancy practice – from those new to the profession to those with many years' experience.

The benefits to be gained are available to all. As a professional body, ICFM assists its members at every stage and in every facet of their professional development. It provides opportunities for continuing professional education, a forum for discussion on issues of common concern, a source of information and a point of contact with other professionals.

The ICFM Certificate of Membership is evidence of the holder's commitment to the Codes and the professional standards set by the Institute. Since membership is individual, it is fully transferable if you change your job. In liaison with other umbrella groups, ICFM also represents members' interests to charities, government, the media and to the public.

ICFM is supported financially by many charities who recognise the importance and needs of the organisation, having become affiliates of its Charitable Trust. Fundraising staff of these affiliated charities enjoy reduced subscription fees. Through its members, ICFM liaises worldwide with allied organisations, such as the National Society of Fundraising Executives in the USA and the Australian Institute of Fundraising, and is represented on the World Fundraising Council.

ICFM aims, through its Trust, to further knowledge, skills and effectiveness in the field of fundraising. It serves the interests of its members, the professional fundraisers, and through them, the interests of charitable bodies and donors. ICFM aims to set and develop standards of fundraising practice which encompass:

- growth in the funds and resources available for charitable expenditure;
- thorough knowledge of proven fundraising techniques;
- new fundraising opportunities;
- cost effectiveness;
- strict adherence to the law;
- accountability.

Other publications from ICFM

Published codes of practice	Member	Non-member
Guidance Notes and Standard Form of Contract for dealing with Consultants/ ICFM Consultants List	£5.00	£10.00
Code of Practice on Reciprocal Mailing	£1.25	£2.50
Code of Practice on Schools	£1.25	£2.50
Code of Practice on Telephone Recruitment of Collectors	£1.25	£2.50
The Scottish Code of Fundraising Practice	£5.00	£10.00
The Use of Chain Letters	£1.25	£2.50
Standard Form of Agreement between Charity and Payroll Giving Professional Fundraising Organisation	£5.00	£10.00
Static Collection Boxes	£1.25	£2.50
Outbound Telephone Support	£1.25	£2.50
House to House Collections	£1.25	£2.50

Published books		
The Complete Fundraising Handbook *Sam Clark*	£11.65	£12.95
Charity Appeals: the complete guide to success *Marion Allford*	£13.59	£15.99
Writing Better Fundraising Applications *Michael Norton*	£8.00	£9.95
Who's Who in Fundraising	£10.00	£14.95
Schools Fundraising *Ann Mountfield*	£8.00	£9.95
Fundraising on the Internet *Howard Lake*	£10.50	£12.95
Review of Tax-free Payroll Giving to Charity	£4.99	£6.99
Reference Manual on Payroll Giving	FREE	£2.50

To order any of the above publications, please contact:

ICFM, Central Office, Market Towers, 1 Nine Elms Lane, London SW8 5NQ Telephone 0171 627 3436/0171 978 2761

Index